Chasing Cheetahs

Chasing Cheetahs

THE RACE TO SAVE AFRICA'S FASTEST CATS

Written by **Sy Montgomery**

Photographs by **Nic Bishop**

Houghton Mifflin Harcourt

Boston   New York

The text of this book is set in Latienne, Laser, and Aram Caps.
Maps and cheetah silhouettes by Rachel Newborn.
See page 76 for photography credits.

Library of Congress Cataloging-in-Publication Data is on file.
ISBN 978-0-547-81549-7

Printed in China
SCP 10 9 8 7 6 5 4 3 2 1

4500445505

TO THE CCF DONORS, STAFF, AND VOLUNTEERS WHO HAVE
GIVEN SO MUCH TO PROVIDE THE CHEETAH A FUTURE.

Contents

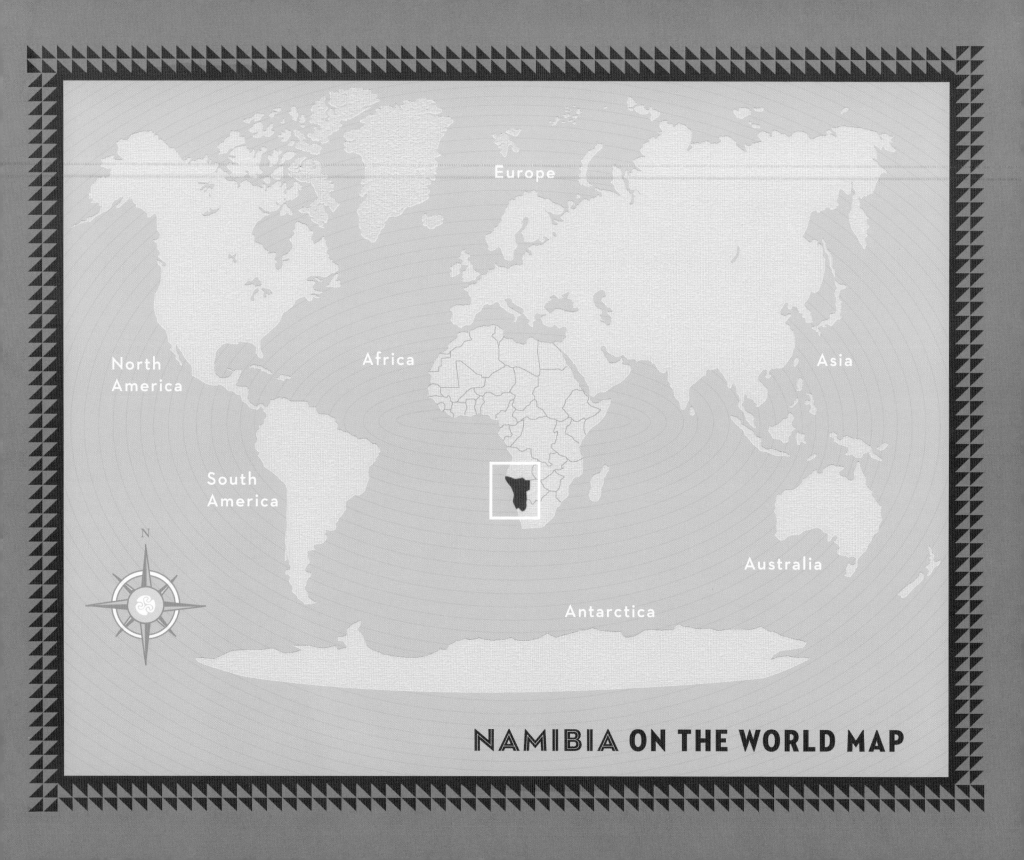

Europe

North
America

Africa

Asia

South
America

Australia

Antarctica

NAMIBIA **ON THE WORLD MAP**

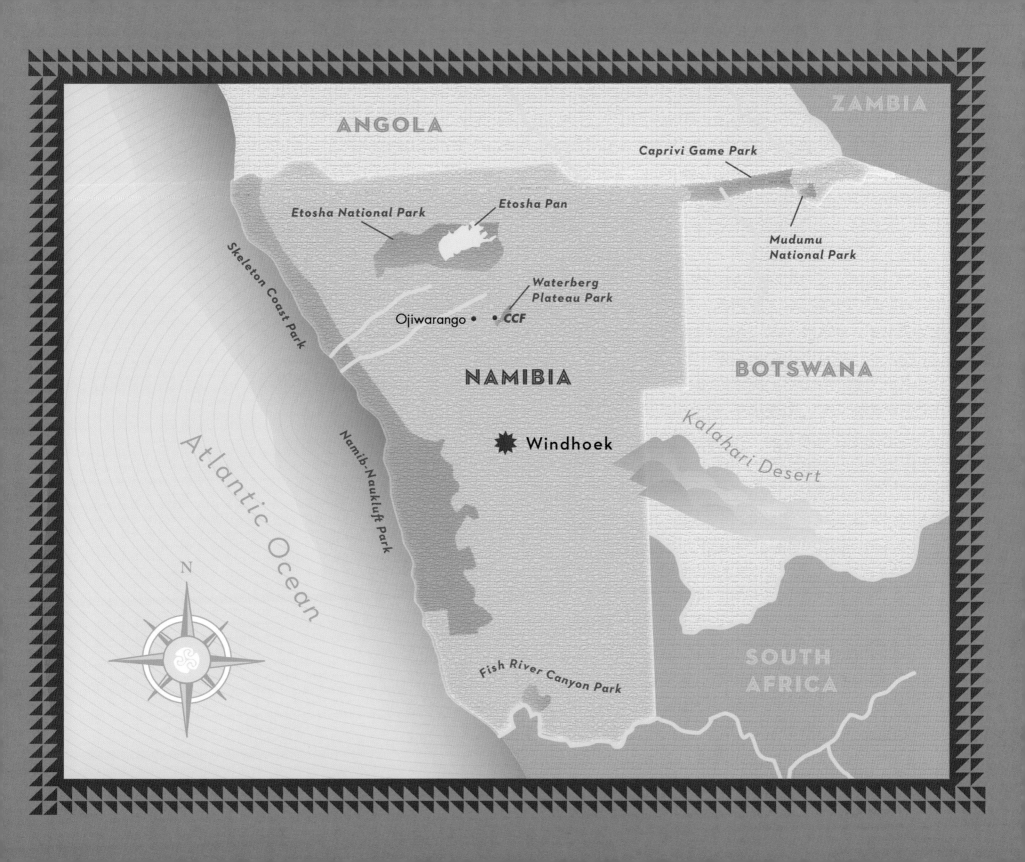

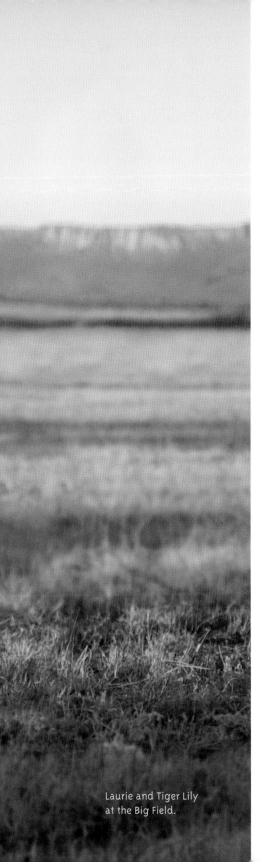

Laurie and Tiger Lily
at the Big Field.

CHAPTER 1

Shortly after we leave the city, the parade of wonders begins: thorny acacia trees hung with the straw nests of weaver birds, like Christmas ornaments; termite mounds as tall as people, pointed like the turrets on sand castles; road signs like those for deer crossings back home, only featuring silhouettes of warthogs and kudu. Along the road, we pass one sign with a crocodile above a crossed knife and fork, advertising a ranch that offers the reptiles for people to eat (instead of the other way around), and another sign advertising the Ombo Ostrich Farm.

Even on the three-hour drive from Windhoek, the modern capital of Namibia (the country to the west of South Africa and Botswana, near Africa's southern tip), we can see we're in for a wild ride. And at our destination, we're greeted by a scene so heart-stopping that it's easy to understand why folks come from all around the world to see it.

A tall, smiling woman dressed in black, her curly salt-and-pepper hair flowing like a mane, is striding toward us—with a ninety-pound black and gold spotted cat at her side. Walking on a leash as calmly as a dog is a predator who

Warthog crossing.

can run as fast as a car races on a highway. It's a full-grown cheetah—the fastest predatory animal on earth, and Africa's most endangered cat.

The cheetah marching toward us is just inches from the woman, and soon the two of them are just yards away from us. A second look brings a sight even more astonishing: behind them are another human-cheetah pair—and another—and another!

"I'm Laurie," says the lady in black, "and this is Tiger Lily."

Laurie has cared for the orphaned Tiger Lily
since she was a cub.

"I'm Eli," says a twenty-one-year-old from Georgia, "and I have Peter."

"I'm Suzie," a young blond woman introduces herself in a clipped British accent. "This is Senay."

"I'm Stephie," chimes in a twenty-three-year-old from Michigan, "and this is Kaijay."

For the lady in black, Laurie Marker, these humans and cheetahs are family. All of them live here at the African headquarters of the Cheetah Conservation Fund (CCF), and they all share the goal that led Laurie to create the organization twenty years ago: to save the stunningly swift and slender cheetah from extinction.

Eli, Suzie, and Stephanie's job as CCF students and staff is to learn as much as they can about a species whose numbers have crashed from more than 100,000 in 1900 to fewer than 10,000 now. The four cheetahs have a different job. As a group, they're known as the Ambassadors. These twenty-two-month-old cats are here to teach humans about the grace and gentleness of these beautiful but persecuted predators.

"These cheetahs came from the other side of the Waterberg Plateau," Laurie tells visitors from Germany, South Africa, and America. She's referring to the orange mountain that is the area's most dramatic landmark. The Ambassadors all flop to the ground at their trainers' feet and start purring, a chorus of contentment worthy of 360 pounds of housecat.

The Ambassadors enjoy an afternoon snooze in the sun.

Their mother, Laurie explains, had killed a farmer's calf—so the farmer killed her and captured her babies. When the Namibian Ministry of the Environment found out, they notified CCF. The cubs were just three weeks old—"little bundles of fur, just starting to walk"—when they were rescued. They were too young to eat meat, so Laurie fed them with a bottle. "It's a lot of work raising cheetah cubs," she says.

At this, Tiger Lily starts licking Laurie's hand with her sandpaper tongue. Laurie rubs her chin. But Laurie stresses, "The point of our work is not to have tame cheetahs. It's to have wild cheetahs."

CCF has rescued more than nine hundred cheetahs, most of whom have been returned to the wild. Some were captured as orphans. Most of them were older than the Ambassadors were when they were caught, and so had

had the chance to learn from their mother for months, not weeks. "That's why there's no way the Ambassadors could go back into the wild," Laurie explains, now straddling Tiger Lily so she can rub the cheetah's ears. Tiger's purring swells like a roaring ocean. "They would want to be with people. They might be able to learn to hunt, but they'd always want to be with people—and that would be a problem."

For most African farmers, a cheetah is the last thing he wants to see on his property—much less walking up to his door. Before Laurie established her organization in Namibia, "farmers were killing cheetahs like flies." Throughout Africa, livestock farmers considered these easily tamed cats bloodthirsty monsters. Even though wild cheetahs never attack humans unless cornered, even though they much prefer wild game to domestic live-

stock, cheetahs were feared and hated as ruthless killers. A CCF survey in the 1980s showed that the average livestock farmer in Namibia killed nineteen cheetahs every year. Humans—not disease, not injury, and certainly not old age—were the number-one cause of death in cheetahs. CCF studies showed that people were responsible for 79.4 percent of all cheetah deaths in the country.

"Cheetahs were considered vermin," Laurie says, as Tiger Lily lies down with a rear leg resting on Peter's neck. Senay starts licking Kaijay's ear. The volume of the group's purring ticks up another notch, and we can feel their contentment rolling in our chests like thunder. "They were like wolves, who are thought of as vermin on many ranches in America."

But the Namibian farmers, like the American ranchers, were wrong. Predators aren't

With a wide yawn, a cheetah
shows off the long canine teeth
needed to bring down prey.

vermin, Laurie stresses. In fact, as studies all over the world have long ago proven, predators are essential to the health of the ecosystem—the ecosystem upon which farmers and their livestock depend.

Laurie knows this firsthand. She has spent more than forty years studying cheetahs, both in captivity and in the wild, and more than twenty years working with African farmers. When it comes to predators, things aren't always as they seem.

Saving cheetahs, she's found, demands re-examining long-held beliefs, asking new questions, finding unexpected answers, and turning enemies into friends. "The problem isn't with predators," she insists. "The problem is with us humans. We have to change the way we think and behave."

Laurie started by working with the folks you might think would be her worst enemies: the cheetah killers. She met with the farmer who killed the Ambassadors' mother. What problems did he face on his farm? How many cattle did he have? How well were they doing? Did he see cheetahs often? Rather than punish him for the murder of the mother cheetah, Laurie listened carefully. She cared about his problems and set about finding solutions.

After talking with the man who had just killed the mother of these cubs whom she

already loved, Laurie ended up giving him a gift: a valuable livestock-guarding dog. With his flock safe, the farmer gave up killing cheetahs.

Laurie's maverick approach to conservation is changing minds and turning heads. She's using dogs to save cats and convincing farmers that killing predators doesn't protect livestock, as we shall see. By thinking outside the box, this white American in an African country has become a powerful voice for hated predators.

As a result, Namibia's cheetah population, once in free-fall, has doubled over the past twenty years to about four thousand. Based on her success, Laurie and her staff have helped develop cheetah conservation programs in South Africa, Botswana, Zimbabwe, Algeria, Kenya, and Iran. Soon she hopes to help reintroduce cheetahs to India. Though they're now extinct on the Indian subcontinent, the name *cheetah* actually came from there; the word is Hindi for "spotted one." Cheetahs were once so common that Indian rulers kept thousands as pets and hunting partners.

For her work, Laurie has been honored with some of the most coveted awards in conservation science, and she was named a "Hero of the Planet" by *Time* magazine. But her work is far from done. Once cheetahs roamed throughout Africa, Asia, and Europe. Now they are confined to twenty countries in Africa along with Iran. Ninety percent of the world's cheetahs are gone. "The cheetah's extinction is happening *now,*" she stresses. "Saving the cheetah actually can be done," she insists, "but only if we can make it happen."

Can we? That's the question that drew the photographer Nic Bishop and me from America to the opposite side of the equator, where June is winter and, even though it's Africa, the cold nights demand wool hats. To bring you the story of the science and struggle behind trying to save this species, we've joined Laurie and Tiger Lily, Eli and Peter, Suzie and Senay, Stephanie and Kaijay, and a cast of other characters, both human and animal, from around the world.

During our stay, we'll work with another forty-five cheetahs that live here, many of whom are learning how to "live wild" again. We'll meet veterinarians, volunteers, and visitors. Our new friends will include students, shepherds, and schoolchildren, as well as some two hundred goats, two parrots, eleven dogs, and one wild cheetah who brings excitement with his regular visits to the compound.

We'll work with some of wildlife conservation science's well-known equipment, such as camera traps and radio telemetry, to figure out where wild cheetahs go and what they do. But we'll also use a surprising combination of other tools—from the machines in a hi-tech on-site genetics lab to a border collie's nose.

Cheetah conservation harnesses many talents and technologies. Saving the cheetah is about more than just one species, one country, and one kind of science. It's about antelopes and birds, leopards and giraffes, soil and trees, dogs and goats. It's about chemistry and genetics, veterinary medicine and ecology. It's about changing the farming system in Africa. "If we can save the cheetah, we can save everyone else

in the ecosystem," Laurie promises the visitors, as Tiger Lily bats playfully at Peter's tail.

"We want to grow cheetah range," Laurie proclaims. "We want to paint Africa with spots again. We *can* save the cheetah," she asserts, "but only if we're brave enough to change our thinking."

As well as being speedy, cheetahs are known to be able to turn and accelerate very quickly to catch prey.

FAST FACTS ON THE FASTEST CATS

- The speediest land animal on earth, the cheetah can run seventy miles an hour, as fast as an automobile on a highway.

- A cheetah can go from 0 to 40 mph in three strides. Each stride may carry a cheetah twenty-five feet.

- The cheetah's flexible spine curves up and down as its legs are bunched and extended, giving the legs greater reach. Like a greyhound's at full stride, when the legs bunch inward, the cheetah's hind legs reach almost past the ears before they fly backwards again.

- Adaptations for speed are similar to those of a greyhound and include a huge heart, an oversized liver, large, strong arteries, and enormous lungs.

- When a cheetah is running, only one foot touches the ground at a time; at two points during its stride, all four feet are off the ground.

- While running, the cheetah may take up to 150 breaths per minute.

- The tail acts as a rudder, allowing for quick turns.

- Claws do not retract into the paws the way other cats' claws do; they remain out like dogs' for better traction.

- Running tires cheetahs fast: the cat must rest after covering only 400–600 yards to avoid overheating.

- Unlike the other big African cats, the cheetah doesn't roar, but chirps like a bird, mews like a kitten, purrs like a housecat (as cougars do too)—and makes many other strange, uncatlike sounds.

- Huge eyes can see detail more than two miles away.

- The cheetah's black "tear marks" curving down from the eyes to the nose probably help reduce glare for better vision. (Though local legend says the cheetah is crying because it can't tell if it's a dog or a cat!)

- A cheetah's nose, with its large nostrils, helps the cat cool down after a chase, but doesn't pick up much scent. Cheetahs' sense of smell is so poor, they may not notice a piece of fresh meat on the ground unless they can see it.

- As in other cats, the cheetah's sensitive white whiskers pick up small changes in air pressure, helping it approach prey undetected and navigate through tight spaces at night. The cheetah's whiskers are shorter and less sophisticated than those of night-hunting cats like tigers, though, because the cheetah hunts by day and can rely more on its excellent eyesight.

Laurie's Story: "Somebody" Was Me

CHAPTER 2

The greatest love story of Laurie Marker's life began with hissing and spitting.

Laurie, twenty years old and living in Oregon, had never seen a cheetah before, not even in a photo. But the minute she held the tiny, frightened cubs born at the wildlife park where she was working, she fell instantly in love despite their angry protests—and her world changed forever.

Now fifty-eight, Laurie remembers it all vividly as she sits in the southern African sunshine on the back patio of her thatch-roofed concrete house at the CCF compound. She and her parents, who are visiting from their home in California, take turns telling the story of how those helpless babies led Laurie from a career as a grape farmer in Oregon to the forefront of predator conservation in Africa.

"We always told Laurie she could do anything if she put her mind to it," Laurie's pretty blond mom, Marline, begins. But as a child, and even as a young woman, Laurie herself could never have guessed how far her mind—and her heart—would take her.

She was sure, though, that her future would involve animals. "Oh, Laurie always loved animals!" her dad, Ralph, says. Growing up near Los Angeles, California, Laurie and her two older brothers spent most of their childhood riding burros and horses. Her best birthday present ever was her first horse, Snap, a strawberry roan, when she was nine. She raised rabbits, adopted stray cats, and refused to go to sleep without her black and white terrier mix, Sox, in her bed.

In 4-H and Pony Club, she spent most of her time on horseback. She learned everything about her pets and kept careful records of how much their food, bedding, and veterinary care cost—an accomplishment that pleased her dad, an accountant. And she loved asking questions. Her mom thought Laurie would grow up to be a scientist. "I think I always was a scientist," Laurie says today. "I was always asking 'Why?'"

Laurie has loved horses since she was a child.

Old family snapshots of Laurie almost always show her with animals.

It seemed natural for her to study science in college. But then Laurie's life took what looked like a big detour when she left college to start a winery.

"I had always thought I'd be a vet," Laurie muses, as her two parrots, Bookie, a forty-year-old lilac-crowned Amazon who was given to her by a Peace Corps volunteer, and Buddy, a twenty-two-year-old Maximilian Pionus she adopted in 1993, scream and beep from her office. (Bookie clearly once lived in a house that played a lot of Pac-Man.) "But in the 1970s, organic farming was *the* thing."

With four partners, Laurie bought land on which to grow wine grapes. She was also raising two milk goats, Goat-o and Toag (that's *goat* spelled backwards). When they gave birth to two bucks, Laurie couldn't afford to keep the boys (males don't give milk, after all). What to do? Happily, the farm was just five miles away from Wildlife Safari, a wild animal park. She went there to donate the little bucks—and ended up with a job at the park's veterinary clinic.

"It all began with goats," Laurie's dad says.

Within a year, Laurie was promoted to the job of clinic director.

Laurie's parents vividly recall visiting their daughter at her new job and seeing how all the animals there loved her. "Even the giraffes would come over and greet her!" her mom remembers. But ever since those first brave cubs hissed and spat at her, Laurie's clear favorites were the cheetahs. "They're the most unique and special animal on earth," she insists. "Nothing else can run seventy miles an hour. Nothing can outrun them. That's pretty special." But she also realized that her cheetahs were racing toward extinction.

Cheetahs were already rare by the 1970s, even in zoos. Cheetahs, unlike lions and tigers, are famously difficult to breed in captivity, even though people have kept cheetahs as pets for millennia. A seal from ancient Sumer (part of present-day Iraq) dated to 3000 BC depicts a cheetah on a leash. From the fifth to the sixteenth century, from Europe to China, kings and nobles hunted with cheetahs, a sport known as coursing. The cheetah, wearing a hood or mask to cover its eyes and keep it calm, would ride behind its human hunting partner on his horse on a pillow, or in a cart, or walk beside the horse on a leash. Once the person spotted prey, he'd remove the cheetah's mask and let it give chase. But of all the millions of cheetahs held captive over thousands of years, the only recorded birth of cubs before the 1950s was a single instance in the sixteenth century. A litter was born to a cheetah owned by the son of Akbar the Great, an emperor of the great Mogul Empire, which once stretched across the Indian subcontinent and beyond. Akbar had kept a stable of *one thousand* cheetahs—probably totaling nine thousand over his lifetime. But only once had they successfully bred, and, sadly, none of the cubs lived past infancy.

Two of the Ambassadors as cubs.

Laurie with Tiger Lily as a cub.

The next birth—in 1956 at the Philadelphia Zoo—was hailed as a near miracle. Over the next two decades, a handful of other litters were born at various zoos. But many of the babies died young. Some were born with two heads or six legs. Others died of kidney and liver ailments, rickets (weakening of the bones), or feline distemper (a viral disease). Nobody knew why the cats wouldn't mate in captivity. Nobody understood why so few cubs managed to survive.

Laurie was among the first to find out. Part of the problem was that most zoos didn't provide the privacy, security, and choice that cheetahs need before they'll start families. In the wild, cheetahs feel secure only when they have places to hide as well as high ground from which to view their surroundings. In the wild, cheetahs choose their mates—females don't breed with any male who comes along. Laurie found that when captive cheetahs have these necessities, they are more likely to breed.

But another part of the problem was more complicated, rooted in a disaster that took place 10,000 years ago.

At the end of the Pleistocene Era, 75 percent of all mammal species in North America and Europe went extinct. Gone were the mammoths and mastodons. Gone were the saber-toothed cats. Once, cheetahs lived in North America (in fact, they originated there) as well as Europe. They died out. But they hung on in Africa and Asia—just barely. Many of the sur-

Laurie has studied cheetahs for more than thirty years.

The Cheetah Conservation Fund's headquarters has a large visitors' center, as well as education and research centers.

vivors were close relatives. When they mated, any genetic problems they had were magnified. Today, African cheetahs are so closely related that you can graft skin from a cheetah from Namibia onto a cheetah from Tanzania and it will grow there fine. This inbreeding is why cubs are born with deformities, why cheetahs are more susceptible to disease, and why cheetahs often have dental problems and tail kinks.

Under Laurie's direction, the cheetah-breeding program at Wildlife Safari became one of the most successful in the world. Her work was so admired that she was hired by the National Zoo in Washington, D.C., where she worked with the International Cheetah Studbook and helped develop New Opportunities in Animal Health Sciences, a research center associated with the Smithsonian, setting the stage for their captive breeding program. Zoos all over the world sought her advice. In 1976 Laurie even took Khayam, one of the female cubs she had hand-raised, to Namibia and taught her how to hunt.

But Laurie knew Khayam was too tame to live in the wild. Khayam became an ambassador of sorts, helping Laurie spread the word about the endangered status of wild cheetahs and the need to protect them. She and Khayam appeared on Johnny Carson's *Tonight Show*. ABC filmed a TV special about the two of them, hosted by the star singer and actress Olivia Newton-John. Winston, Oregon, displayed a bronze statue of Khayam in the middle of town.

But nobody was stopping the slaughter of cheetahs in Africa.

"I thought if I told enough people about the threat to cheetahs, they would take care of it," Laurie says. "But they never did. They were always saying, 'Somebody ought to do something about cheetahs,' but I could never find out who 'somebody' was."

Until she looked in the mirror and realized, "'Somebody' was me."

She sold everything she owned in 1991 and moved to a borrowed farmhouse in rural Namibia, where 20 percent of the world's cheetahs live. She started visiting farmers and asking them questions. How often did they see cheetahs? Did the cats attack their stock? What were the farmers doing to protect their animals?

Their answers led Laurie to a surprising conclusion: "The way to save cheetahs isn't by keeping them all in national parks. The way to save cheetahs is by working with people." Most of Africa's cheetahs live on privately owned

land—and in Namibia, that means livestock farms. Saving cheetahs, Laurie has found, can't be done without understanding farms and farming in the countries where cheetahs live.

Today Laurie's conservation research center in central Namibia includes a state-of-the-art genetics laboratory, a sparkling new veterinary surgical suite, and an inviting visitors' center, which welcomes thousands of people a year. She and her husband, the population geneticist Dr. Bruce Brewer, manage a staff of nearly eighty people from around the world. Forty-five cheetahs live here, many of whom are learning to live again in the wild with the help of their human keepers.

But nothing at the center is more important than the two hundred goats. "It all started with goats," her dad reminds us, and goats are still a big part of the picture.

"The way to save cheetahs," Laurie insists, "is all about goats and dogs."

She promises to show us why tomorrow.

Meat is snatched as soon as it is thrown into the enclosure.

Saving Cats with Dogs

CHAPTER 3

"We've got cheetahs everywhere," Laurie told us as she showed us around the center. "Down here, over there," she said. She pointed to the grassy pens, which enclosed fifteen, fifty, even two hundred acres, all with trees and mounts from which the animals can view their surroundings. "Cheetahs are all around you!"

We were eager to meet those cheetahs. At feeding time, we got our chance.

"Come, girls! Come, come!" Juliette Erdtsieck, CCF's cheetah curator, guns the engine of the HiLux pickup as she calls out the window in a clipped South African accent. "Hello, Rosy! Hello, Nina!" Juliette honks the horn. To the cheetahs, that's a dinner bell. They lope along behind the fence next to us, easily keeping up with the truck. They know the back is filled with horsemeat (coated with "predator powder" for extra vitamins and minerals), and chasing it—and then eating it—is the highlight of their day.

"Clever girls! Good girl, Solo! Good girl, Misty!" calls Juliette. The cheetahs almost screech to a stop when we reach the end of the fence. Juliette hops out of the truck and unloads stainless steel bowls and chunks of meat.

Some cheetahs chase their meal by running behind the food truck.

The cats wait by the "guillotine gate" (it doesn't cut their heads off, just slides up and down like a guillotine on ropes operated from outside) to be let into the feeding pen. The cheetahs are impatient. Hissing and spitting, stomping and swatting, they make unearthly sounds that sound like a cross between an alley cat in heat and a vacuum cleaner choking on a rubber glove.

Feeding time is all hisses and snarls.

Intent on food, this cheetah
is ready to pounce.

With the meat distributed in the bowls and Juliette safely outside the pen, she hoists the gate. Cats spurt inside as fast as water from a fire hose. Each rushes to a bowl, grabs a piece of meat, and starts running again—as if capturing prey. Then they each trot back to a bowl, drop the meat into it, and begin to feed.

Why feed the cheetahs in a bowl? Because they'd eat out of one in the wild, says Juliette. The bowl in the wild is the carcass! The hair, skin, and body cavity of the dead animal holds the meat in one place and keeps it from collecting dirt and grass.

The cheetahs bolt their food. "They eat fast because they're at the bottom of the predator chain," Juliette explains. Lions, leopards, and even hyenas and jackals will drive a cheetah off her kill and steal it. "Cheetahs have to eat fast and move on."

We move on, too, because there are lots of cats to feed. The Leopard Pen (it once housed a rescued leopard, now released) holds four male orphans, Anakin, Obi Wan, Omdillo, and Chester. They're exceptionally vocal as they await their meal, hissing and yowling, snarling and swatting. It doesn't bother Juliette a bit. "Hello, gorgeous! Hello, love!" she greets each one cheerfully. "This is the proper sound of a cheetah," she tells us, "what you want to see in a wild cat." The four make scary sounds and erect their hair to make them look larger—to show, explains Juliette, "'I'm strong. I'm fast. I'm mean.' That's what you need to ensure you don't lose everything to the other wild preda-

tors." At Bellebenno, the soft-release camp we'll visit later, these four male orphans have learned to hunt together successfully. They will soon be released to Erindi Game Reserve.

Each cheetah has a story. Each begins in tragedy. After a farmer shot their mother, Rosy and her sister were confined to a four-by-six-foot cage with no water and only rotting jackal and baboon meat to eat until their rescue in February 2003. Kayla and Kiana had rickets—a vitamin deficiency from being held captive as babies. Shadow, a small, dark cheetah with a stalking gait, had been captured by a farmer as a cub with her mother and siblings. They were rescued and released—but Shadow was captured again by a different farmer and sold to a private owner. By the time she was rescued a second time, she'd become so shy, she hid constantly. Today, though, living in Eland Pen with females Dusty, Blondi, and Sandy, Shadow comes forward eagerly at feeding time, ears forward, coat shining with health.

Back near the research center, we watch as Stephanie and Suzie feed the Boys. N'Dunge—which means "smart" in Oshiwambo—was so named because, unlike the others, he holds his meat down with a paw to anchor it while eating. He lives with his lighter brother, Shunga ("blond"), Little C, and Ron in a pen next to the Ambassadors. On the other side, with penmates Rohini Talalla and Polly, live Hermione and Harry, named for the Harry Potter characters. They're such good friends that they groom each other after feeding, licking blood off each other's faces, purring loudly with pleasure.

But there is one cheetah whom we didn't meet that day: Hi-Fi.

We'd already heard about him, though. At our first breakfast, eaten with staff outside at long metal tables (where we were told to avoid the large termite mound near the kitchen, since a colony of Africanized bees and a spitting cobra live there), we heard he'd been spotted the night before. A sheet posted at the research center ("Hi-Fi: Have You Seen Him?") recorded recent sightings: Stephanie glimpsed him slinking behind one of the captive cheetahs' pens at 5:35 p.m.; a volunteer saw him sitting in the grass by the water tower at 6:50 and again at 8:05 p.m.; an intern from Oregon watched him walking near the picnic area at 7:30 a.m.

Laurie told us the staff started seeing him near the center four years ago with his brother. The two were captured and radio-collared on Namibian Independence Day, so they were named after Namibian presidents. (Hi-Fi is mercifully short for Hifikepunye Pohamba, the current president; his brother, Sam, was named for the founding president, Dr. Sam Nujoma.) Sadly, in 2010, Sam was found dead of wounds probably sustained while hunting. Hi-Fi is still a regular visitor, if an elusive one.

Nic and I were eager for a glimpse of him. "If he sees you, he just walks away, then turns and looks at you," Laurie said. Nobody here is worried that a large, wild, predatory cat regularly walks among us. "When we see him, we say, 'Oh, it's just Hi-Fi,'" she explained.

Cheetahs don't attack humans. But what's really extraordinary is that on CCF property, Hi-Fi also comes within easy hunting distance of the herd of two hundred sheep and goats. The wild cheetah just walks right on by.

That Hi-Fi lives peacefully among them proves the power of one of Laurie's surprising ideas for cheetah conservation: using dogs to save cats.

The mysterious Hi-Fi is occasionally photographed by camera traps set up beside play trees and animal trails.

Hi-Fi is snapped by a camera trap as he sprays a fence post with scent markings.

"Hi, Kiri!" Laurie bends down to pet the friendly cream-colored dog and rub around her dark floppy ears. Laurie doesn't have to bend far; Kiri is a Kangal dog, a huge breed native to the Anatolian region of central Turkey, where her kind has been guarding sheep from wolves, bears, and jackals for six thousand years. Thick coats make these dogs look even bigger than their 90 to 150 pounds.

Kiri's ear massage is cut short by a wet nose. A young brown and white French Alpine goat nudges Laurie's arm, while a white bearded Saanen goat nibbles at her black pants. "Hello, girls," Laurie says—only to be mobbed by goats, bleating and nuzzling. She points out four who were born just yesterday. Seven more moms are expecting kids next week. "Hi, babies!" she says to the little ones. "How are you?"

Laurie makes her way through the crowd to introduce us to one of her old friends—a dog named Shades. The big male is twelve years old, and his dark face is grizzled with white. He wags as Laurie approaches. "How do you like the babies?" she asks him. "The babies like *you!*"

A Kangal dog will fiercely defend the stock it guards, yet it is always loyal to and gentle with its human owners.

Laurie explains how good livestock care can help reduce the number of cheetahs being killed by farmers.

Indeed they do. Dogs like Shades and Kiri are the best friends a goat could have—as CCF's flock of healthy goats and sheep testify.

Next we meet the man whose job it is to spread the word. "A dog this big, a cheetah will not challenge," says Gebhardt Nikanor, a CCF staffer who works with farmers to educate them about the benefits of these big, brave, loyal dogs. "If he does, he would go away with injuries or even death. And the dog has a big voice also," he says. A bark that deep and fierce can drive even a leopard away.

That's why CCF has been breeding dogs since 1994 and offering puppies at low cost to goat, sheep, and cattle farmers. The big dogs instantly reduce stock losses to almost zero.

"People have used dogs to protect livestock for centuries," Gebhardt explains, "but these dogs are bigger and able to scare away larger predators." They stay with the livestock twenty-four hours a day. One dog can look after as many as two hundred goats.

Though a dog seldom has to do more than bark to scare predators away, each one stands ready to protect the flock with his or her life. That's because CCF raises the puppies with their own goats and sheep. To dogs like Kiri and Shades, goats and sheep are like family.

By the time a farmer collects a pup at two months old, the dog already understands he's part of the flock. "Any dog has to be trained," says Gebhardt, "but these dogs' instincts are so good, you don't need much training." The pups are valued at two to three thousand Namibian dollars ($1 U.S. = $8 Namibian), but CCF offers them for seven hundred Namibian dollars, so that even farmers who are not well off can afford them.

Not just any farmer can get a puppy; Gebhardt makes sure they go only to farms where cheetahs roam. (Some farms have only small predators like jackals and caracals, against which Namibian African dogs will protect livestock easily.) Each farmer who applies is carefully screened. CCF staff visit the puppy three times at his new home the first year, and once a year thereafter. The farmer signs a contract promising that CCF can withdraw the dog if he's not being cared for properly. CCF has placed more than four hundred dogs on Namibian livestock farms, and there's a two-year waiting list for pups.

The nineteen dogs here, and the two hundred goats and sheep who help train their pups, have some of the most important jobs in cheetah conservation, Laurie says. With their flocks safe, farmers don't need to kill predators. They'll let cheetahs come and go on their property, free to hunt the wild game the cats prefer. When the farmer who killed the Ambassadors' mother was given one of these dogs, says Laurie, he was transformed from a cheetah's worst enemy to a cheetah's good friend.

Laurie leans down to stroke Shades again. "We've been through a lot of changes together," Laurie says to her old friend, "haven't we?"

The pups are raised with goats
or sheep and learn to guard
them as if they are family.

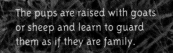

THE GOATS WHO HELP TRAIN FARMERS

Many visitors, when they see a herd of goats at the cheetah center, assume the animals are there as food for the cheetahs. The thought is gruesome, but it makes Tyapa Toivo laugh. "We'd be out of goats in about a week!" he says.

Tyapa, who has a bachelor's degree in agricultural management, is in charge of the goat yard, and he knows the goats have a much more important job to do than provide lunch for the cheetahs. At first the goats were there to train the dogs. Now they're training farmers, too.

In just the past four years, CCF has hosted more than three thousand student farmers. They come for a free week-long course designed especially for "communal and emerging farmers," folks who want to start farming but haven't had any training.

Why should a cheetah conservation organization train farmers in keeping goats? Because, Tyapa explains, a healthy flock is less likely to attract the attention

of a predator, and a farmer who's barely making ends meet is more likely to take out his frustration on cheetahs.

So Tyapa, along with Gebhardt, teaches farmers how to build corrals to protect vulnerable newborns. They discuss finances. They tell farmers about proper veterinary care and the importance of good food and clean water. They use the goat yard here as a model, where young farmers can see how a farm

should look. It's neat and clean, the goat yard is fenced, and gates are fitted with locks because, as Tyapa says, "Goats are smart. They learn how to open the gate!"

CCF's goats and sheep help underwrite the cost of the training programs as well as the steep discount the farmers get on pups. The sheep are hardy Damaras or fat-tailed sheep, a breed that thrives in the desert and sports handsome, curling horns. They are sold for

Armas protects his goats
with the help of his dogs.

Each morning, Armas takes the herd out to graze.

meat, while the female goats produce gallons of creamy, healthful milk that buyers eagerly pay a premium for. (Many people with allergies to cow's milk can drink goat's milk safely.) CCF staff members make and sell goat cheese and goat's-milk fudge. They're even experimenting with rich goat's-milk ice cream. The flock here illustrates how well-cared-for animals and innovative new products can make a farm more profitable.

One of the best investments a farmer can make, besides a dog, is a herder to keep the goats and sheep together when they leave the paddock to graze. "The dogs don't herd—they guard," explains Tyapa. "Though if a single goat or sheep is left behind, the dog barks to alert the herder."

Today that would be Armas Shaanika, who has worked with CCF for fifteen years. We accompany Armas and Tyapa, dogs Amos and Ushi, a handful of sheep, and about 180 goats (the fifteen now giving milk and the smallest babies stay behind) as the *baa*-ing herd flows out of the corral gates to graze the green and golden grasses of the savannah.

Armas carries a red paint can, which he bangs with a stick to urge stragglers along. Walking among the contented flock as they nibble is a good job, he told us, "peaceful—just you and the dogs and the goats and the wildlife."

Though born in northern Namibia, Armas has lived here most of his fifty-five years. Like half of all Namibians, he speaks the Oshiwambo language. Tyapa translates for us as Armas explains that he was one of the first lucky farmers to receive one of CCF's shepherd pups. That female, Mondessa, changed his life, he tells us. He never had to worry about cheetahs anymore. Today his own flock of fifty-five goats is guarded by two CCF dogs, Shepherd and Cheetah. "They are my protectors," he tells us. The dogs mean far more to him than livestock; they are more than pets. "They are like my employees," he says.

Laurie and a play tree.

Messages Written in Scent

CHAPTER 4

Two days after our arrival, we awake to discover that a drama has unfolded while we slept. Nobody is sure when it happened. All we know when we emerge from the guesthouse in the morning is that all the cheetahs are running around, very excited.

With excellent reason, as the staff soon discovers. For at the edge of their pen, females Harry, Hermione, Van, and Polly are eyeing the carcass of a nearly four-hundred-pound antelope!

How had the unlucky beast ended up there? Laurie pieced together the story from the fence, which was broken in three places (and very quickly repaired by Bruce).

This was clearly the work of Hi-Fi.

"Hi-Fi has been especially interested in the Girls lately," Laurie explains. He's been seen hanging around near their pen and marking nearby trees with his scent, hoping to attract their attention. "He's frustrated," she says.

But something took his mind off romance last night or early this morning, at least for a moment: an adult male oryx, one of the largest

A large oryx can weigh four times as much as a cheetah.

common antelopes in central Namibia. Who could resist chasing him? But bringing down a four-hundred-pound antelope with three-and-a-half-foot-long, lancelike horns isn't easy. But "predators are smart," Laurie says, "smarter than we give them credit for." That's why Hi-Fi didn't kill the antelope. He let the fence kill the antelope for him.

Three times Hi-Fi drove the oryx to crash into the fence. The third time, the fence broke the oryx's neck. Laurie says Hi-Fi knew exactly what he was doing. And if he had been trying to impress the captive females, this would have done the trick!

At 9:45 a.m. we check on the carcass, hoping for a glimpse of Hi-Fi. He's gone, but we can see that he has eaten the left shoulder—

Finn's extraordinary sense of smell is crucial to the team's success.

evidence that our ghostly wild visitor is still nearby.

The visit from Hi-Fi makes us wonder all the more: What's life like for a wild cheetah? Where do they hang out? What do they eat? How do they stay in touch with other cheetahs?

To find out, Laurie works with a team of ecologists. Laurie rounded them up for our outing from their offices at the Haas Cheetah Research Center. At their desks on the second floor, we find the chief ecologist and a native Namibian, Matti Tweshingilwa Nghikembua; Eli, Susie, and Stephanie, whom we've already met; and Finn.

Except Finn's "desk" is a dog bed. That's because he's a border collie—a breed ranked as the smartest in the world.

"Finn is also an ecologist, because he's equal to Eli and Matti, Steph and Suzie and me," Laurie insists. He's an essential part of the team, and without him, we'd be missing one of the most sensitive pieces of equipment in our scientific toolkit: his nose.

Finn has been trained to find and show us cheetah poop. His skills are crucial to discovering how wild cheetahs use the landscape here, and even which individual cheetahs visit specific areas. It's not an easy job. Cheetah scat—or poop—can look just like leopard scat. Plus it's not always in an obvious place. But Finn

has trained for years to do his job—first at the Philadelphia Zoo, learning from the poop of captive cheetahs there, and for the past three years here at CCF.

He sniffs out cheetah poop the way other dogs sniff out bombs or drugs. Once he finds it, a human staffer can collect it and analyze it in the laboratory, and find out whose it was, whether male or female, find any parasites, analyze its hormones, and discover what the cheetah was eating.

Today we're headed to some places cheetahs particularly like. We park the two pickups by Chewbaaka's Field Tree, named after one of Laurie's favorite cheetahs—a handsome, friendly male who, until he died at age sixteen on April 3, 2011, served as CCF's chief cheetah ambassador. Chewbaaka used to sniff this tree carefully whenever he visited it. He'd leave his scats for other cheetahs to find. And because the stout trunk leans at an angle, he could easily climb it.

A thornless tree with small olive-colored leaves, the species is called a shepherd tree, Matti explains, because it's so useful to shepherds: they eat the fruits, chew the leaves to cure night blindness and headaches, and flavor yogurt with the roots. But cheetahs, says Laurie, use the tree to leave messages for one another—messages written in scent.

Eager to work, Finn whines to be let out of his crate in the back of the pickup.

"Ready?" Laurie asks him. Finn's white-tipped tail whips madly. "Find!"

Finn heads straight for the scat and sits down so Suzie can collect it for analysis. Finn is wearing a radio collar in case the researchers need to track him. You can see the antenna sticking out near the base of his right ear.

Lots of animals frequent trees like this one, Matti says. At fifteen different trees he's studied, camera traps, programmed to snap photos when animals cross an infrared beam, have recorded visits from cheetahs, leopards, porcupines, meerkats, and aardvarks (night-loving animals with the snout of an anteater, the ears of a rabbit, and the body of a pig), among others. Many species poop here. But Finn ignores the scat of other animals. He beelines to the base of the tree and sits down emphatically. There, just to his right, is a fresh pile of cheetah poop.

"Got some? Good boy!" cries Steph. As his reward, she fishes out a blue Kong toy from her treat pocket and throws it. He races after it, overjoyed.

Meanwhile, Suzie dons plastic gloves, collects the scat in a baggie, and labels it with the

Eli and Matti measure
Chewbaaka's field tree.

date and location in order to take it back to the lab.

"This is a five-star tree!" says Matti. Farmers have known for years that certain trees attract lots of cheetahs, and for that reason called them "play trees." "They thought cheetahs came to play here," Matti explains, "but that's a misconception."

What do cheetahs *really* do at these trees? How often do they go there—and why? What makes a play tree so attractive? Answering these questions will be the focus of Eli's project.

Building on Matti and Laurie's years of study, Eli will measure just about every variable he can think of. What species of tree is it? (Not all play trees are shepherd trees.) How fat is the trunk?

Does the tree lean? At what angle and in what direction? Does climbing the tree give the cheetah a better view? How big is the canopy? What are the surroundings—grass, bush, a road, a track?

Eli needs to take lots of measurements. For most of them he can use an ordinary tape measure, recording his data in the scientific metric system. For some he needs a compass. And for several he needs human helpers. How do you measure how well a cheetah can see from a tree like this one? The first measurements are taken from cheetah height (about three feet from the ground). Choose a random direction on the compass and send a companion—Suzie in this case—walking till you can no longer see her, and then measure that distance. Next, go

up into the tree and again, from the height at which a cheetah would be standing, find out how far you can see your colleague. Then try again in other directions.

The next play tree, another shepherd tree, is just a short walk away. It's called Field 1 Tree, and Finn is eager to go there. "We're going to find more—are you ready?" Laurie asks him, though she already knows the answer.

"Find!" says Steph. Together we follow Finn down a red dirt track. A light wind brings Finn a symphony of scent. He turns right and sniffs at a depression in the dirt.

"What?" asks Laurie. But she knows what it is. This is a scrape—an area where a cheetah scuffed his back feet into the dirt, leaving scent

Matti sets up a camera
trap to record visitors to
the play tree.

Hi-Fi's visit to yet another tree
was recorded by a camera trap.

from glands between the toes. But there's no scat here, so Finn moves on. He reaches the base of the tree and pointedly sits. Beside him is a very old cheetah scat. He draws his lips back and lets his pink tongue hang out in a dog smile. He gets another toss of the Kong toy. "You did great!" says Laurie. "You're a good boy!" echoes Steph.

"This is a good place to set up a camera trap," says Laurie. There are two of these special cameras in the car. Suzie quickly lashes them to two posts in the ground, to record cheetahs from two angles. From the patterns of spots, they can usually tell individuals apart. "I wonder if we'll get a picture of Hi-Fi?" Laurie says. "I want to know where he hangs out!"

One place Hi-Fi is known to frequent is Field 2 Tree, and we drive there next. A camera-trap photo once recorded Hi-Fi standing on two legs here, his front paws on the tree's stout trunk. It's a camel thorn acacia, a big tree that can live to great age, with pods that many animals like to eat. But no cheetah could climb this particular tree, as it's not angled at all. There's a big termite mound nearby, where small animals have left scat. But no cheetah has left any fresh poop here today. Finn seems disappointed. So Stephanie hides some "practice scat" she brought with her in the car and asks him to find it. He does, immediately—and is rewarded with another toss of the blue Kong toy.

Getting long-term data on the play trees around CCF's land will build on studies the CCF has been working on for years, says Laurie. It will take hundreds of thousands of measurements from dozens of different trees to show just what makes a play tree so special to cheetahs.

But there are two mysteries that we might be able to solve in a matter of days. Who left the scat by Chewbaaka's Field Tree? And what was he or she eating?

To answer the first question, we'll need to visit the genetics lab.

TAKING THE MEASURE OF A TREE

Here are some of the measurements we took of Chewbaaka's Field Tree:

🐾 Diameter of trunk at human waist height: 108 centimeters (cm)

🐾 Height of tree: 350 cm

🐾 Farthest branch to farthest branch in one direction, then its opposite: 4.9 meters and 5.4 meters, respectively

🐾 Crown diameter (calculated by multiplying pi [3.14] x 4.9 divided by 2, x 5.4 divided by 2): 20.8 square meters

🐾 Distance of tree from a road or a track: 13 meters

🐾 Angle of incline (using a mathematical formula to determine ratio of length to height): 28 degrees

🐾 Compass direction tree is leaning in: 70 degrees from true north

🐾 Visibility at cheetah height from play tree: 29 meters

🐾 Visibility at cheetah height from ground at play tree: 29 meters

Laurie records the data.

By climbing a play tree, a cheetah can use its keen eyesight to gaze far across the surrounding plains.

Cooking with Poop and Toasting Hair

CHAPTER 5

side of this door

Janine puts the DNA samples into the genetic sequence analyzer.

Janine Fearon dons her white coat and sterile gloves and heads to a well-stocked freezer. "We've got boxes and boxes of poop," she says, as proudly as any chef showing off her larder. She easily finds the carefully labeled sample from yesterday.

Then, like a hostess cutting crusts off bread for tea sandwiches, she shaves off the crust on the outside of the poop. But instead of throwing it away, this "crust" is the prize. This is where the DNA is, shed from cells in the cheetah's intestines—and this will give us the information we'll need to find out which cheetah left the scat at Chewbaaka's Field Tree. Janine scrapes it off with a sterile scalpel onto a sterile surface. Even though we're working with poop, the lab is as spotless as the cleanest test kitchen.

Janine and a CCF master's student, Lucia Mhuulu, will spend much of today and tomorrow doing what chefs do—measuring, mixing, and cooking. "It really is like a recipe—in which the secret ingredient is poop!" Janine says.

Janine and Lucia start the process by breaking down the scat sample to release DNA.

In fact, growing up on a farm in South Africa, Janine wanted to be a chef. But in high school she switched to science. She loves nature, and as a conservation geneticist, she's proud to be gathering the data that will tell Laurie which cheetahs visit which areas—and help Eli figure out why.

"You think of wildlife and nature," she says, "and you think of David Attenborough. But a lot of people don't understand that all wildlife research also involves many hours of work in the laboratory. We make a lot of conservation decisions based on genetics. For instance, if you look at genetic diversity, you can see which species or populations are the most threatened—and you know where to put your priorities."

Cheetahs should be near the top of that list, she says, because of their dangerously low genetic diversity—a problem discovered thanks in part to technicians like herself and Lucia, working toward her master's degree in genetics at the University of Namibia.

The recipe they're following today gets pretty complicated. There are lots of weird ingredients you'd never find in a supermarket (is Proteinase K on your family's shopping list?) and equipment that sounds like something a comic-book superhero might need (like the super mixer vortexer and the thermocycler.)

In this "kitchen" the DNA in the cells is spun, heated, cooled, and copied. It's all part of the process to get the DNA to give up its secrets.

Lucia further purifies the DNA sample.

SECRETS OF DNA

Like many good secrets, the mysteries of DNA are written in code.

The instructions for all life are written in a code of just four letters: A, C, G, and T. Each letter stands for a chemical called a nucleotide. Like a single letter of the alphabet, each nucleotide means nothing by itself. But as with letters strung together to make a word, the order in which the nucleotides appear in the DNA molecule is what matters.

DNA is too small to see without special instruments and computers, but if you could blow it up big it would look like a twisty, spiraling ladder. The rungs of the ladder are the important parts. Each rung is made of two nucleotides that always pair together. Adenine (A) always pairs with thymine (T). Guanine (G) pairs with cytosine (C).

The sequence of nucleotides in DNA gives the unique instructions for making each living creature—a cheetah, a person, a snail, or a pine tree. A cheetah's DNA code is more like a cougar's than a snail's. The DNA codes of sister cheetahs Senay and Tiger Lily are more similar to each other than they are to, say, Blondi's or Shadow's. That's why DNA can show you who's related to whom.

But even though closely related individuals' DNA codes are similar, everyone's code is unique. You don't even have to read the entire code to tell who's who; sometimes just a small part of it can give you the information you need. That's what we hope to end up with tomorrow, after all that mixing and cooking is done, Janine explains. The genetics lab keeps a list of the important parts of the DNA codes of all the cheetahs whose scat or blood they've ever collected. By comparing the code in this scat with that list, Janine and Lucia can tell whether the cheetah who visited Chewbaaka's Field Tree is one of the more than twenty cheetahs they know from the area—or if it's someone new.

Animal DNA has many secrets to tell us.

Janine and Lucia proceed with the recipe:

Measure 600 milliliters of lysis buffer (a chemical that will rip the cells apart to get the DNA out of the scat sample). Add to sample. Mix together in the super mixer vortexer. Spin (at 12,000 revolutions per minute) in centrifuge. Remove liquid from top. Add neutralizer tablet, return to super mixer, then spin in centrifuge for six minutes. Add Proteinase K (an enzyme to further break down the cells). Bake at 70 degrees Celsius for ten minutes.

Two more trips to the centrifuge and—voilà! At the end of the day, the DNA is ready to be copied, a process with its own recipe for adding enzymes, primers, and water and its own schedule of heating and cooling. It will take at least one more day before the DNA is ready for another superhero machine, the genetic sequence analyzer, run by a powerful computer—which will give us our answer.

But meanwhile, in a small room in the research center next door, we can solve our other mystery: what our cheetah was eating.

Veterinary technician Rosie Glazier explains how to begin: the process of solving this mystery starts with poop in pantyhose.

To get a scat to reveal what a particular cheetah has been eating, first you need to wash away the dirt and plant material on the surface, and all the products of digestion, Rosie tells Janine, Lucia, Nic, and me. Next, put your sample into one foot of the pantyhose. Then tie the foot shut, wash the pantyhose in the washing machine in the barn (not the one for clothes!), and dry it on the line like regular laundry. Once it's dry, you've got a light, golf-ball-sized mass of hair, bone, and sometimes feathers. "Now for the fun part," she says.

Rosie unties the washed and dried pantyhose

and, with tweezers, selects ten of the largest, longest, most complete hairs for examination. She puts aside the first candidates on a sheet of white paper.

Each hair she selects gets to be the filling of a "hair sandwich." She places a single hair on a clean glass slide, tops it with a clear plastic cover, and on top of that adds another glass slide. She presses it all together with special clips and pops it into the toaster oven at 108 degrees Celsius. In five minutes the "hair burning" is complete.

"What burning does is transfer the hair's scale pattern onto the plastic cover," Rosie explains. "You're not going to look at the actual hair under the microscope—just the impression of its surface." That's because the hair itself is too thick for light to penetrate sufficiently to reveal the intricate pattern.

Even a single hair can convey a great deal of information.

Under the microscope, at just 10 times magnification, we can see a surprisingly complex pattern on the hair's surface, like the tiles in a mosaic or the panes of a stained-glass window or the scales of a fish. And luckily for us, the pattern is different for the hair of each animal species— so different that we can tell whose hair is in the scat of our mystery cheetah the way you would identify a bird or a flower by using a field guide.

Like most field guides, the one Laurie developed for animal hair uses what's called a dichotomous (die-COT-o-mus) key, which means "in two parts." Each set of two questions or statements describes two mutually exclusive possibilities.

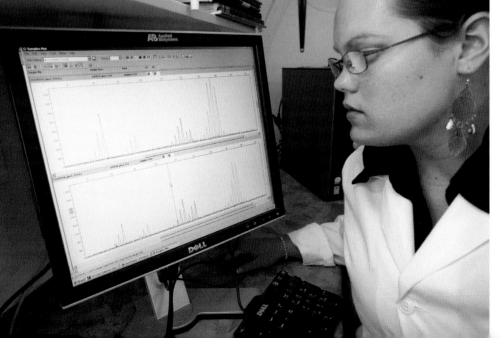

At the end, the DNA code is displayed by a computer and matched against samples from other animals in order to identify the owner.

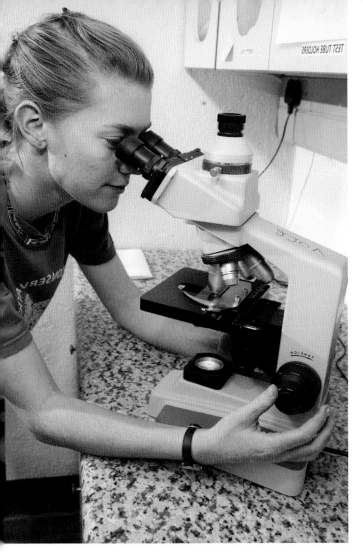

The hair is identified from its unique surface patterns.

A chameleon cautiously marches across open ground as it searches for a new tree to climb.

("Is it bigger than a breadbox? Or not?") Your answer to the first set of questions leads you to a second couplet—and so on, until finally you have an ID for your species.

Answering the questions isn't always easy. The first is "Is the pattern pectinate? Or not?" Our guide shows nine different, mosaic-like patterns to choose from. Some are wavy; some look like stones set in concrete. "Pectinate" looks like skinny diamonds piled atop one another. After taking turns at the microscope, we agree this one doesn't look pectinate.

On to the next question. "Is it regular mosaic? Or not?" We look at the picture showing regular mosaic and agree our sample is not. "Is it regular waved? Or not?"

The picture of regular waved looks just like our hair.

"Is it irregular at the tip?" That is, does the pattern hold at the very tip of the hair, or does it change? We agree that it changes. It's irregular.

And that answer leads us to the final dichotomy: "Do the scales get closer and closer together at the tip? Or not?"

We look carefully and decide: not. Good thing! Had the scales been closer and closer together at the tip, that would have meant our cheetah was an outlaw—because that hair pattern is for the wool of a sheep!

But no. Our cheetah had been eating exactly what a wild cheetah ought to: a medium-sized brown, black, and white gazelle, known as a springbok.

But which cheetah ate the springbok? The lab won't have the result till tomorrow evening.

In the meantime, we're presented with a mystery that's far easier to solve. The next morning, another dead oryx turns up near a different cheetah pen, the one right next to Laurie and Bruce's house, the pen that holds the three very tame, four-year-old cheetahs known as the Stars—Quasar, Soraya (Persian for the the Pleiades, or Seven Sisters, constellation), and Phoenix.

The cheetahs were, of course, quite interested. It seemed as if antelopes were showing up like pizza deliveries.

And it was pretty clear who the deliveryman was: none other than our mysterious friend Hi-Fi.

Game Drive

CHAPTER 6

Whether you're a cheetah dining on an oryx or a scientist lunching on a sandwich, mealtimes are exciting at CCF.

Dinner's the best time to catch up on who last saw Hi-Fi and where. At breakfast, we watch cheeky hornbills steal unattended toast. At lunch, parades of spotted guinea fowl hunt bugs in the grass. Warthogs kneel on their front knees, munching leaves. Sometimes Tripod, a male warthog with a lame back leg, ventures close; he knows he's safe near us. Nic and I love that while we're eating, the animals are eating, too.

For us, meals are easy. Our sandwiches or soup, breakfast cereal, or dinner casseroles are laid out, buffet style, inside the cement and thatch building that houses the kitchen where Agnes the cook presides. But for wild cheetahs, each meal can be a life-or-death challenge—if you're even able to get a chance to eat at all. This afternoon, still awaiting an answer from the genetics lab, we're headed out to the Big Field to see what might be on the menu for wild cheetahs.

Every month since 2004, CCF staff members have conducted regular, careful game counts along different routes—not only to keep track of cheetah food, but also to check on the health of the entire ecosystem, Matti explains. The checklist includes antelopes such as eland, oryx, kudu, and steenbok; predators like hyenas, cheetahs, and jackals; birds such as kori bustards, guinea fowl, red-crested korhaan . . . twenty-three species of commonly seen animals. It's not the complete list of everyone you might see out here, so there's a space for "other" on the sheet. "All species are ecologically important," explains Matti, "but the reason we picked these is that they are all indicator species"—meaning that their presence or absence can indicate the health of the ecosystem—"and most of them are huntable," and therefore vulnerable to overhunting.

THE CRUCIAL ROLE OF PREDATORS

Predators, such as cheetahs, wolves, and polar bears, inspire us with their strength and skill and delight us with their beauty. But predators, even tiny ones, are more valuable for the role they play in keeping the world healthy and whole.

What happens when an area loses its predators? Only recently have scientists begun to catalog the cascade of disasters that befall an ecosystem when predators disappear. Here are just a few examples:

🐾 In the 1970s, overhunting of sea otters in the Aleutian Islands off Alaska turned an undersea forest into a desert. Sea otters love to eat sea urchins, but when hunters killed all the otters, the spiny creatures bred out of control. Sea urchins eat giant kelp, marine algae that grow underwater as tall as trees and as densely as rainforest. A kelp forest is one of the richest habitats on earth, supporting hundreds of species, from diving birds to strange and beautiful fish. But without the sea otters to keep the urchins' numbers in check, the urchins ate all the kelp, and all the other crea-

tures disappeared too. Happily, once overhunting was stopped, the otters returned—and so did the kelp and the species that depend on it.

🐾 In a Venezuelan valley flooded by construction of a dam in the 1980s, Duke University ecologists noted that the top predators—jaguar, mountain lion, harpy eagle—fled the rising waters. Even armadillos left the area. Only a few islands of high ground remained. But howler monkeys, living high in the trees, stayed behind. With no predators to hunt them, the howlers multiplied rapidly. Soon they ate almost all the plants on the islands, leaving only the poisonous and thorny ones. But even these succumbed to the disaster set in motion by losing the predators. With no armadillos to eat the leaf-cutter ants, their population exploded. The ants carried so many leaves down to their underground nests that they starved the soil of nutrients.

🐾 In the busiest section of Utah's Zion National Park, the crowds of human visitors scared away all the cougars. Then, researchers discovered, the cou-

gars' main prey, mule deer, became so numerous that they ate all the baby cottonwood trees growing on the banks of the rivers. Without the cottonwoods to anchor the soil, the banks eroded, clouding the water with dirt. Fish, amphibians, and streamside plants like rushes and willows died in turn. The researchers noted, though, that nearby North Canyon still has its cougars—and fifty times more cottonwood trees, along with a healthy ecosystem for species ranging from red-spotted toads to bright red cardinal flower.

🐾 Even the loss of tiny predators can have a big impact. Yale University ecologists tried an experiment. They removed the spiders from selected patches of a field and then watched for over three years to see what happened. Without spiders, the field changed, right down to the chemistry of the soil! The effect depended on the kind of spiders that had lived there. The researchers found that the spiders that actively hunted grasshoppers, not surprisingly, kept the population of grasshoppers down. Grasshoppers eat grass and goldenrod, so more grass-

Many predators have adaptations that allow them to hunt particular types of prey. The cheetah has exceptional speed and agility, making it an effective predator of small antelopes.

hoppers meant fewer of these plants, which in turn decreased the amount of nitrogen, a plant nutrient, in the soil. But removing the spiders that used a different method of hunting—stalk and ambush, hiding in wait to surprise a passing grasshopper—caused a different change. It altered the *behavior* of the grasshoppers, which changed the plants, which changed the soil in a different way. When the spiders were there, the grasshoppers would hide in the goldenrod instead of eating the grass. But when the spiders were gone, the grasshoppers could breed out of control and eat anything they wanted—creating a less diverse plant community and soil with more nitrogen.

"Everything is connected to everything in nature," observes Howard Quigley of Panthera, an organization devoted to saving the thirty-six species of cats on earth, including cheetahs. Removing the predators, he says, "has impacts we're just now scratching the surface of."

Overhunting isn't the only factor affecting game numbers. Bush encroachment is another. When big browsers like elephants and rhinos disappear, thorny bushes replace grasslands. Thorns hurt cheetahs' eyes as they chase prey into the bush. Today 12 percent of Namibia's landmass—some 34 million acres, more than three times the size of Switzerland—is so thick with thornbush that no one can live there.

CCF is working for the day the elephants and rhinos come back. But until they do, CCF hires workers to clear some of the thornbush. At their factory nearby, they make the plants into a long-burning, almost smoke-free fuel called a Bushblok, which is sold to city dwellers and lodge owners in Namibia and South America.

The list of factors affecting the numbers of game animals is a long one. "If you see fewer antelopes, there could be a disease. If you see too many, that means there are no predators," says Matti. A drop or rise in game numbers can tip off ecologists to a change affecting the entire ecosystem. So it's important to keep track.

You need at least four people to do the game count. One person drives. At least two count the animals (one set of eyes on each side of the car). Another person records the time, number, and location of each animal spotted.

It's a difficult task, especially in the Big Field. "Big Field Road is always busier than the rest," says Matti. "Everyone has their favorite routes. This is mine. It used to be a maize field. Now look at it!" No longer a flat expanse of corn, it's flecked with small acacias, spiky aloe plants, a mix of grasses, and minty-smelling blue-green bitterbush. It offers good visibility, and also places for wildlife to hide. So we're lucky to have many pairs of eyes watching today. Along with Matti, Nic, and me, we have six seniors from Cape Henry Collegiate School in Virginia Beach and their chaperone, Paul Horgan. The students chose Namibia as the site of their senior class trip, and they'll return to the States just in time for graduation next Sunday.

We make a left onto a track marked Middle Field Road. "With carnivores, the easiest way to see them is on camera traps," Matti continues. "But with herbivores, this is the easiest way. Though smaller ones—steenboks, duikers, warthogs—are lower in the grass...

"The most important thing I can tell anyone learning game count," Matti tells the students, "is *be patient.*"

Game drives can be time-consuming, but Matti loves the chance to watch animals.

Seniors Greg Noordanus and Lexi Decker from Cape Henry Collegiate help spot animals in the Big Field.

TOP: If cornered, a warthog can inflict serious injuries with its tusks.

ABOVE: Small antelopes like this steenbok are favorite prey for cheetahs.

At 3:35 p.m., we stop. "No more talking," Matti warns. "The animals are listening." And then, quietly, his already soft voice just above a whisper, he explains what to do.

"We will split into left and right teams," he says, "on the left and the right side of the car.

We'll have one person who's the recorder." Lexi Decker, her blond hair in a ponytail, volunteers and is given the checklist.

"One person gets the range finder." Greg Noordanus, one of the seniors, volunteers, and Matti hands him the tool. It focuses like a binocular. "Point it at an object," says Matti, "say, that acacia tree. Focus. Then press and hold this button, and it will tell you how far away the tree is." Greg does, and announces the distance as the range finder measures it, in meters: 97. (A meter is 3.28 feet.) "If we find a group of animals," says Matti, "take the reading of the animal in the middle.

"Ready to start?"

But before he drives even ten yards, we have animals to record. "Warthog!" a tall boy in a black T-shirt points out. "There's a baby, too!"

"Thirteen meters!" Greg says.

"That's good!" says Matti. And because the students are so calm and quiet, the mother and piglet don't run away.

"Bird!" A girl sees it from her seat in the vehicle's second row. The creature is right in front of the car. "A black korhaan," Matti says. "It's a male." Lexi writes it down.

"Oryx, two o'clock!" observes a student. Greg notes it at 256 meters, and Lexi records it.

"Bird on Termite Mound—and he's busy killing something!" says Matti. It's a hawk, not one of the animals we record, but it's exciting to see a predator in action as he starts eating the rodent he's just captured in his talons.

"Warthog to the left! There's three—or four? Looks like a mother and her young ones…" says a girl with a brown ponytail.

"Oryx on the left, 215 meters…I think there are three at least," says a girl in a blue headscarf.

"Wow, they are doing good!" says Matti admiringly. "I love doing game counts. Every one is different…You never know what you might see!"

Matti points out a camel thorn acacia along the truck, old and twisted. On a game count last year, he and his colleagues saw a leopard there. "What we did not know was that the leopard was lying in ambush for a warthog and her two babies," he tells me. "When our car came, the leopard jumped down, all the warthogs were spooked by us. The next thing was—explosion! I slammed on the brakes. Piglets are running. The mother is unhappy. The leopard is growling. And then he caught one of the piglets! It happened so quickly! The other piglets ran back to this side of the road, and while we heard the piglet he caught screaming, the mother warthog was coming to defend the baby. But the leopard was growling—the sound they make is a weapon. The growl was so loud you could *feel* it in the car! No matter what you want to do, you won't be able to do it with a leopard growling. So the mother warthog ran off." The leopard got his meal.

"Something big! Way out!" A boy in a blue T-shirt shoots out his arm to point. Paul, a chaperone, calls out *Ostrich!* It's a handsome black and white male, our first sighting of the world's largest bird. Ostrich can't fly, but they can run forty-three miles an hour (impressive, though no match for a cheetah's seventy). Their long legs can cover sixteen feet with a single stride and are powerful enough to kill a lion with a single kick. "And two oryx!" adds Paul. "Both male. And four more ostrich on the right!"

Students are spotting species almost as fast as Lexi can write them down. We're all thrilled that we're actually seeing them and that they're here at all. Since the counts began in 1996, Matti says, the number of animals seen on game drives has markedly increased. And three years ago, he started seeing something remarkable: the return of predators.

When Matti, who grew up in Namibia, started working with CCF as an intern in 1997, things were different. "I never thought I'd see a cheetah close up unless it was trapped by farmers," he says. "And now we have a wild cheetah who even comes into the center! Hi-Fi is a very good signal there is peace."

It's not only cheetahs that have staged a comeback. Other predators, from leopards to jackals to the caracal, a small, secretive cat with lynxlike ears, are returning too.

Many oryxes later, at 4:03 p.m., we spot a fox-sized animal running away from our car. It's a creature few of us have ever seen before, even in a book, with stripes like a tiger and the body shape of a dog. What is it? "Keep your eyes on it…" says Matti, "don't lose it . . .

"You guys, it's an *aardwolf!*" he cries with excitement. It's a kind of small, furry hyena, rarely seen but hated by farmers. Though aard-

A mongoose family peeks from the safety of long grass.

wolves don't kill livestock (they actually prefer insects), farmers trap and poison them throughout their range in southern and eastern Africa because they think aardwolves kill lambs. Greg's reading shows the aardwolf twenty meters to our left. It swivels large ears to catch our murmurs, stares at us with black, alert eyes—then lopes away like a wolf.

The *wow*s sweep through the car like waves on a shore.

Back in camp before dinner, we stop at the genetics lab to see if Janine and Lucia have our answer. Is our Chewbaaka Field Tree cheetah an individual the research center has recorded before? Or is it someone new?

Janine is almost as eager to tell us as we are to find out. "It's someone we know!" she tells us. Who? She can't keep the secret any longer: "It's Hi-Fi!"

CONSERVANCIES: SHARING THE WEALTH OF WILDLIFE

Prior to Namibia's independence, in 1990, almost all of the country's wildlife belonged to the government—a government the people eventually overthrew. Except for the rich private landowners, people had no rights to use wildlife and no financial incentive to protect animals. Poaching was rampant: by military forces during the independence struggle; by commercial poachers looking to sell meat, heads, and skins; and by people who killed animals because there was nothing else to eat. Perhaps 10,000 cheetahs were killed in the twenty-year period before independence. Many areas of the country had no wild animals left at all.

But six years after coming to power, the new Namibian government changed its wildlife policy. In 1996 it gave most of the country's farmers the rights to profit from the wildlife on the land they worked. To exercise these rights, they had to form conservation organizations known as conservancies.

In a conservancy, adjacent farms or tourist lodges get together and plan how to manage the land while restoring and protecting the wild animals who share the land. They can charge people fees to visit a lodge on the land and see the wildlife; they can hunt some of the game and eat it or sell it to others. But whatever they do, they have to preserve the animals' overall numbers. And everyone in the conservancy must share in the profits.

What happens when land is managed in this way? An official report from the government concludes: "Wildlife recovers. Poaching pressure disappears. Plains game reappears." Conservancies have been driving a steady increase in wild animals across the country, including cheetahs.

More than 80 percent of Namibia's wildlife—and most of its cheetahs—live outside of national parks. Namibia has what is called a dual land-tenure system, meaning that almost everything outside of state-protected areas is controlled by private landowners or by communally owned farms. "That's why conservancies are so important," Laurie insists.

When people work together to protect wildlife, everyone wins. Providing better habitat for wild animals means there's less pressure on predators to turn to livestock for food. People collaborate on building roads, managing water, controlling fires, and fighting poaching and other crimes. Pooling the knowledge and resources of many people provide better opportunities for tourism. Coordinating management plans means that instead of competing, everyone's working toward a shared goal.

Among conservationists, Namibia today is famous for its conservancies. The nation boasts sixty-five communal conservancies, covering about one-sixth of the nation's land area but soon to cover more than a fifth, and twenty commercial, or private, conservancies. Today about 40 percent of Namibia's land is set aside as conservation areas. Most of it is protected by conservancies.

Laurie is proud that CCF's land is part of the Waterberg Conservancy, the second communal conservancy in the country, protecting 444,789 acres of

land—more than half the size of Rhode Island. The conservancy's cooperating managers share strategies for creating popular tourist lodges (guests love to see more wildlife) and successful farms.

After all, if wild prey animals are abundant, predators won't hunt livestock. "If people value wildlife," Laurie says, "everybody benefits."

The Cheetah Conservation Fund's land is part of the Waterberg Conservancy, which surrounds the Waterberg Plateau, seen in the distance.

Boot Camp for Cheetahs

CHAPTER 7

Ryan Sucaet holds the antenna out the window of the Land Rover and presses the receiver to his ear. "I think Bella's going to be near here," he tells us.

With Rachel Shairp, Ryan has been tracking Bella and another female cheetah, Padme, since sunrise. "They're doing great," Ryan tells Laurie. "They're finding prey, the right kind of prey, and the right amount of prey. I'm proud of them!"

Ryan is a recent graduate of Michigan State University. Rachel, after her stint in Namibia, is headed for a master's degree in her native England. But Bella and Padme are students too—at a school for cheetahs. Their classroom is this fenced, eight-thousand-acre former game reserve called Bellebenno, where they're learning to be wild cheetahs again.

Ryan and Rachel like to check on each cheetah at least twice a day. "They came in so young. They've all been through so much," says Rachel. Padme, now four, came as a seven-month-old orphan. Bella, now five, had been captured as a cub by a farmer who confined her to a chicken coop. "Most of our cheetahs saw their mothers shot. Captivity has been their whole life," Rachel explains. "To be out in the wild again might be quite an adjustment."

That's why Laurie developed a "soft" release program. After all, for these orphans, the lessons a mother would have taught them were cut short. So rather than release them directly into the wild, orphaned cheetahs at Bellebenno can hone wilderness skills under the watchful eyes of human helpers.

The place has plenty of cheetah food: eland, steenbok, warthog, kudu, oryx, hartebeest. And here the cheetahs may get a chance to meet competitors, too: they're sharing the classroom with brown hyenas and leopards, whom they must learn to avoid. But "this way we can limit the stress and see if they can do it—in an environment where they can be helped and constantly monitored," Ryan explains.

Thanks to telemetry, both radio-collared cheetahs should be easy to find.

"I want to see Bella," Laurie says. "Let's get out of here."

Rachel, Laurie, and Ryan at
the Bellebenno boot camp.

We step carefully off the track and into the bush. "Watch out for warthog holes!" warns Ryan.

"And thorns!" says Laurie.

"And snakes!" adds Rachel.

The magic hour for finding snakes is between nine and ten a.m.—right about now. Twelve species of poisonous snakes live in the area. Just yesterday, Nic and I met a puff adder—a handsome snake that injects a very potent venom from big folding fangs. Eli had discovered the snake while he was cleaning the Ambassadors' enclosure, ushered him into a large garbage bin, and moved him out to the bush. During one morning's tracking, Rachel saw her cheetahs move off and soon discovered why when a thick, dark snake reared up to sway in front of her face. Only later did she

The puff adder is one of the most dangerous snakes in Africa because it often lives close to people's houses and is very hard to see.

learn it was a black mamba, one of the deadliest snakes in Africa.

"We're definitely getting closer," says Ryan. Good thing; our pants and socks are covered with burrs and thorns. Nic and I see why Rachel's and Ryan's clothes are in shreds.

"This is near where Bella caught the steenbok on her fourth day," says Rachel. "All of her kills were made near this road. Maybe she's caught something!"

Bella and Padme were released on May 23, a week and a half before Nic and I arrived, and since then they have both made successful kills. Usually Ryan and Rachel discover this when they find a cheetah feasting on a carcass. But just last week, Ryan was lucky enough to see Bella kill a small antelope called a duiker. He was tracking her with an American volunteer, Bill Young. "She was in a dusty clearing surrounded by dense bush," Ryan recalls, "and this duiker appeared three meters away. I was writing in my notebook, and Bill tapped me: 'Look at this!' Bella sprang to her feet and sprinted eighty meters through the dense bush. We followed the death cries of the duiker till we caught up."

Normally a cheetah trips its prey with a front paw, then bites the windpipe to strangle it quickly. But Bella was still learning. "At first, the kill took her a while," Ryan explains. "She wrestled the duiker for five minutes. It would get up, stunned, and she'd pin it back down. And finally she got it by the throat, as we watched from twelve feet away." He was so proud—"proud and

honored," he said. "It's not easy for them. But they let us sit here and watch."

Suddenly Laurie stops short. "Oh—there she is!" she says. We see Bella twenty yards ahead, sitting beneath a camel thorn acacia. "Hello, Bella! How are you doing?" she says.

Bella rises to her feet, staring at us with her high-set, enormous eyes. Her intense orange gaze seems to sweep over the savannah like light from a sunset. And surely that gaze is taking it all in. No other land mammal's sight is so sharp; only hawks' and owls' vision is more acute.

Now we can see a three-inch wound on her left shoulder. Ryan explains that this is probably from the tusks of an angry mother warthog whose baby Bella had been hunting the week before. They didn't see it happen. But at 11:30 a.m. yesterday, they saw Bella come upon a family of warthogs, two adults with three piglets. Bella caught a piglet in her mouth. The baby squealed. As the mother approached, Bella dropped the piglet, unharmed. "She had it by the back of the head and could have easily carried it off," says Ryan. But the cheetah paused to look at the mother warthog, and let go—perhaps remembering the encounter that had left her wounded. For Bella, says Ryan, "it was a lesson learned."

We're happy to see her wound healing nicely. Rachel and Ryan still supplement the cats' diet with meat and have been hiding antibiotics in Bella's food.

"It's a difficult transition," says Ryan, "especially for females, because they hunt alone."

Ryan tunes in to Bella's radio collar.

Bella is well on her way to learning how to survive by herself.

Male cheetahs hunt in cooperating groups called coalitions, as lions do. Together they can take down larger prey and subdue even big animals before any of the coalition members get hurt. Females may hunt alone because they need to be extra secretive to protect their cubs.

(When left behind in the den in the first six weeks, many cheetah cubs are killed and eaten by other predators, including lions, leopards, hyenas, or even baboons.)

But one group of orphaned females defied the rule: Chanel and the Chocolate Girls. Chanel, born in May 2000, arrived with her two brothers at CCF in May 2001 after their mother was shot on a game farm. Nestle, Hershey, and Toblerone were born in July 2002 and were orphaned at six months. After acing boot camp, they were released at the privately owned Erindi Game Reserve just as 2011 began.

Erindi's 195,206 acres make Bellebenno look like kindergarten. The leopards, lions, and aggressive spotted hyenas that live there will steal cheetah kills and also kill adult cheetahs. But Chanel and the Chocolate Girls didn't know that. The lodge's ranger watched in astonishment one day as the all-girl coalition not only chased two lionesses away from their kill but actually attacked the much larger cats—who were so shocked by this uncheetahlike behavior that they ran away!

"They were wonderful, those four!" said Ryan. Sadly, in late 2011, Nestle was found dead, likely speared by the horn of an oryx. And in early 2012, rangers at the game lodge watched in horror as Toblerone was kicked to death by an ostrich.

But the story doesn't end there. The two surviving females, Chanel and Hershey, have since been seen in the company of males—and both may be pregnant.

🐾

"You look good, Bella," Laurie says to the cheetah. "Now let's go find Padme."

Laurie, Ryan, and Rachel are more worried about Padme. She has made fewer kills than Bella, and she sticks closer to the roads. We drive north along the track, and now Padme's signal is strong. "She's got to be right in here…" says Laurie.

We get out and pick our way through the holes and thorns as Ryan consults the telemetry. The antenna got damaged when he fell into a warthog hole last week, so its signal is less emphatic than usual. It sounds less like a beeping heart monitor and more like the inside of a seashell you listen to at the beach. But soon we see Padme, sitting down and peering out at us from behind a termite mound, about twenty-five feet away.

She stands and moves toward us, moaning like a lost ghost as she approaches. She doesn't like it that Nic and I are here. But she keeps coming, licking her lips, and thinking of meat—meat that Rachel and Ryan didn't bring. Her voice grows louder and more plaintive as she peels back her lips to snarl and hiss at us. It's as if she's saying, "Don't come any closer to me—but give me some meat!"

She stops ten feet from us. We back away.

"I'm sorry, sweetheart," says Ryan.

She is hungry and fearful at once.

"Obi Wan was her brother," Ryan tells Nic and me. "We released him and he did great." Obi Wan, Padme, and Anakin all came to CCF around the same time and were named after Star Wars characters. Obi Wan was one of the Leopard Pen Boys, along with shy, dark Anakin, large, aggressive Omdillo, and Chester, a cheetah who arrived in 2008 with a broken left rear leg, a casualty of the trap that caught him.

The Leopard Pen coalition was released to Bellebenno last November and stayed in the wilderness, like Jesus, for forty days. They learned to hunt, find water, and avoid competitors. They were returned to the Leopard Pen after they caught the scent of some CCF females in a distant pen. They beelined to the neighborhood and wouldn't leave, apparently too enthralled with the ladies to hunt anymore. But Ryan thinks they are excellent candidates for release into the wild.

Surprisingly, after rehab at CCF, Chester proved to be the best hunter of them all. "To go from having a broken leg to being such a successful hunter surpassed everyone's expectations," Ryan tells us. "It was an amazing thing to see!"

That's why Rachel and Ryan don't mind living in tents at remote Bellebenno, facing snakes, thorns, and no showers for weeks on end. "I have the easy job," says Ryan. "I just follow the cats. They have the hard job—to learn to hunt and be wild again."

As we leave Padme behind, she stops hissing and snarling. If she's going to have meat today, she'll have to hunt it on her own. "Not every one of these cheetahs will be able to be wild again," says Laurie. Those who don't—like the Ambassadors and the Stars—still live healthy, interesting, long lives. "But at least," adds Rachel, "we're giving them the chance to find out."

Hungry, Padme approaches us, while warning us not to get too close.

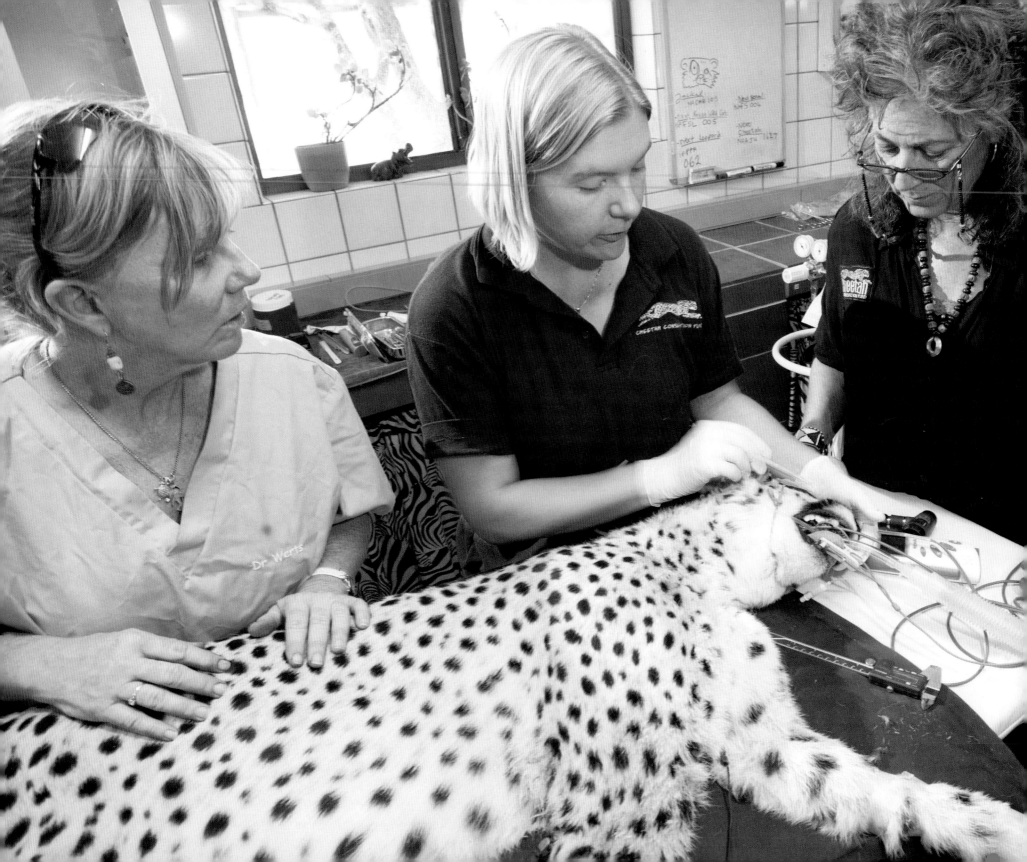

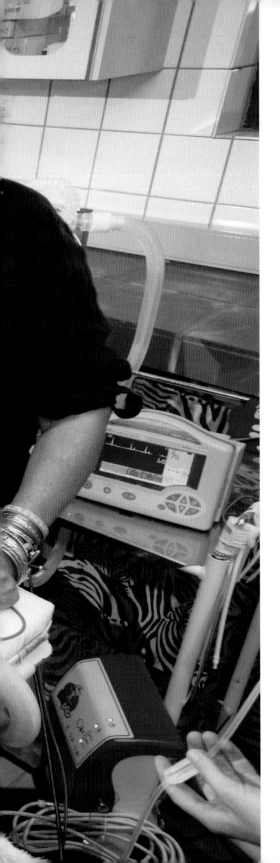

Blondi at her physical exam.

CHAPTER 8

Gaby Flacke, an American veterinarian, opens the dart-gun case. She's already loaded the dart with a cocktail of tranquilizer drugs. Now she attaches the needle to one end and a hot-pink fluffy to the other end to stabilize its flight. She slips the assembly into the dart-gun chamber, adjusts the pressure, and starts walking toward Blondi, a very large female cheetah named for her yellowish coat. She has a distinctive black speck on the lower half of her left iris, and when she's waiting for her food, she makes a special chirping sound.

Blondi doesn't like the look of the dart gun one bit. She lets out a snarling moan, the cheetah equivalent of "Oh, no!"

"She knows," says Laurie. Blondi came to CCF with her sister Dusty (named for her darker, spottier fur) in August 2000, when they were three-month-old orphans. Blondi has been through this before. But Laurie still tries diplomacy. "It's so nice to see you, Blondi," she says. "We're not going to do anything bad to you…"

In fact, we're darting Blondi to keep her healthy. "When I started in the 1970s, the average lifespan for a cheetah in captivity was thirty-six months," Laurie says. "Many didn't do well in zoos. But we've learned how to keep them healthy." Blondi is twelve years old now, and she's in excellent condition for her age in part because she gets yearly veterinary check-ups like the one we're about to do today.

Blondi begins to run back and forth along the fence. "It's all right, love—calm down," Juliette offers soothingly.

Gaby takes aim and fires.

The dart hits the cat in the shoulder. "Sorry, Blondi," Gaby apologizes. The cheetah runs, then trots, then staggers. In fifteen minutes she is lying on her side. Gaby and Juliette squeeze moisturizing drops into her open eyes and then drape them with a blue blindfold. "If she jumps up," Laurie calls to another visiting vet and volunteer waiting outside the pen, "close the gate."

Luckily, Blondi doesn't jump up. Gently lifting her by the legs, four staff members move her from the ground to a stretcher and hoist her onto the back of the truck to take her back to the clinic.

After getting ready, Gaby and Laurie begin Blondi's checkup.

As in a human operating suite, at the clinic the patient is surrounded by people, each performing a different job. Gaby inserts a tube down Blondi's throat to make sure she breathes well. Laurie draws a blood sample from a rear leg for testing. Rosie shaves Blondi's front leg so that the visiting vet Mathieu Werts can insert a small catheter into a vein to deliver fluids and more tranquilizer. During the exam, her heart rate and the oxygen level in her blood are monitored constantly. "Heart rate is eighty," Rosie announces reassuringly.

"She looks good for her age," says Laurie.

Small flies begin to flutter out of Blondi's fur. These are cheetah flies. Like mosquitoes, they snack on blood, and can be irksome. Not all cheetahs have them—it often depends on the season of the year, the region where they live, or even their particular pen. Two volunteers from Earthwatch, a Massachusetts-based organization that pairs paying volunteers with science projects around the world, come to the rescue. Their job is to catch the flies as they crawl out of Blondi's fur and pop the heads off

before they infest the clinic. Their reward is a chance to stroke her fur, which is surprisingly coarse. One person compared it to Astroturf! But it's lucky these cats aren't soft like snow leopards, for instance. At least cheetah fur isn't in demand for rich people's coats.

Juliette looks in Blondi's mouth. "Want to do the teeth?" Gaby asks her. Blondi's in for an exam and a little bit of cleaning, just like your annual checkup at the dentist. Cheetahs get tartar just as people do.

Several of Blondi's front incisors are broken, which isn't unusual for an old cheetah. Gaby calls out a report on each tooth as she examines it, while Dr. Wertz makes notes in Blondi's medical records: "Mandibular incisors: worn, fine, and fine. Tip of left canine is worn but no root exposure…" More worrisome is the big, pointy right upper canine tooth, the root of which is exposed. "Bacteria can get in and she can get an abscess," explains Gaby.

What do you do about a cheetah with an infected tooth? The same thing you'd do for a person. A root canal is in Blondi's future. But that will have to wait. The dentist in the nearby town generously offers his services to all of CCF's cheetahs when in need. "He loves working on cheetahs," says Laurie. No wonder: their teeth are really big!

"Let's do some abdominal ultrasound action," Gaby suggests next. With the clinic's new ultrasound scanner, she wants to check the belly organs for lumps or scars. The kidneys are of special concern. Like housecats' kidneys, cheetahs' kidneys are prone to damage, because their diet is high in protein, so the kidneys have to work extra hard. With an ultrasound probe, Gaby can see and measure both kidneys as easily as a doctor can see an unborn baby inside the mother. "Right kidney," she announces, "6.39 centimeters long and 3.49 wide. Healthy and normal—a good size, a good shape." The left kidney is in fine shape too, measuring 6.87 and 4.03 centimeters. With the probe, she checks the bladder (empty), liver, and spleen—all fine.

Gaby checks Blondi's teeth for wear or infection.

Meanwhile, the cheetah flies vanquished, the Earthwatchers, Judy and Shannon, have begun Cheetah Spa. As the others continue the exam, the two retired law officers comb through Blondi's coarse fur and remove every burr, every thorn, every tangle. Laurie trims Blondi's claws. "We used to joke about this," says Laurie. "What if all the girl cheetahs we'd captured got together and compared notes? They wake up all groomed and trimmed, and they all have new ear tags and radio collars, like earrings and necklaces! They'd ask each other, 'Did you meet these people who knocked you out and took you to a spa?'"

"Pulse is steady," announces Rosie.

Some x-rays show that Blondi's lungs are clear and healthy. Next we check her tail. Kinks are common evidence of genetic damage, and we want to see if she has one. We slide our hands in loose fists down her long tail, and there it is, just at the tip. We can feel the kink as clearly as a small rock lodged in the pocket of your jeans.

At 3:24 we turn her over and do her other side. "We used to try to do these exams with nothing," remembers Laurie. When she started CCF, she had no vet, no equipment—just a stethoscope and some vaccines and her own good eyes. But now, thanks to generous donors, the clinic is state of the art, and Blondi's annual exam is more thorough than many humans'. The data gathered on her health will add to the impressive trove CCF has amassed about a previously little-known species.

By four p.m., it's all over. "She's got two broken teeth and needs root canal—but otherwise, she's good," Gaby announces. We load the sleeping cheetah gently back into a crate, and half an hour later, we release her back into her pen. She will probably remember nothing of the probes and scans or the many loving hands combing her fur, trimming her nails, and stroking her tail.

Happy about the successful exam, Nic and I, Laurie and Bruce, and three friends visiting from the States are hanging out by the Ambassadors' pen when Juliette comes running in with the news.

"Hi-Fi's out there!" she says. "Over by Eland Pen!"

We jump in the car and speed over. "There he is!" says Laurie.

Our hearts pound. This feels like seeing a celebrity—a shy one who avoids the public and the paparazzi. We meet at last!

Nic and I are impressed. Even though he's a hundred yards from us, it's evident that Hi-Fi is a huge cheetah. When Gaby changed his radio collar last year, she weighed him: he was nearly 120 pounds, the largest cheetah CCF had ever recorded.

At the sight of our vehicle, Hi-Fi slinks off to his left. But soon he sits and turns, calmly watching us with those huge sunset-colored eyes. When we next spot him, he's fifty yards away, sitting sphinxlike in the thick bush, not far from where the oryx delivery happened two nights ago.

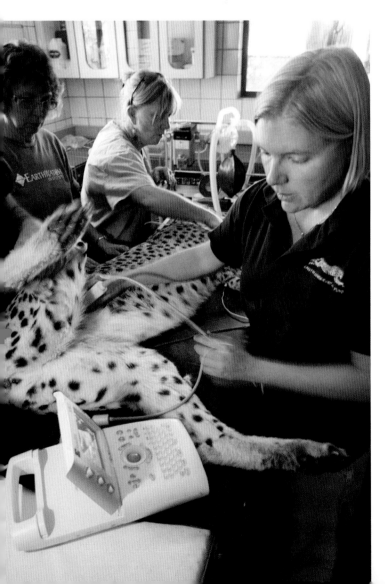

Ultrasound is used to check the kidneys and other internal organs.

Hi-Fi pauses to stare at us; then he is gone.

But if you blink, he disappears. Or seems to. Because his spots make perfect camouflage, Hi-Fi is invisible—until he moves. Slowly, silently, he creeps off into even denser bush. And then he stops, turns, and looks at us. "He's right here!" Laurie whispers. She and Nic get out of the car and approach him quietly, to within forty-five yards, forty, thirty-five, thirty...

The rest of us watch through binoculars. Hi-Fi's tail twitches with tension as Nic snaps photos. "He'd probably like it if we didn't bother him anymore," Laurie says.

Nic and Laurie turn back to the car. "He's lived with us all these years," Laurie says, "and he never goes for the goats. It's just amazing. He's a great cheetah. All these years together, and we all live in harmony." Nobody worries that a cheetah is loose on the property—quite the contrary. His presence among us is proof that CCF's maverick approach to conservation is working and that predators and people can live together in peace.

That night, around the fire, Matti sings a song for us that he has written about Hi-Fi, a tune as soft as a cat's paw. The lyrics give words to the unspoken conversation between this gentle, elusive cat and the humans who are just as curious about him as he is about them. In part, the song goes like this:

> *I will be coming to check on you*
> *No matter how often they mark me.*
> *In the darkest night*
> *You'll see me.*
> *Oh, you are so beautiful*
> *Near me, yet so far away...*
> *Till the next night—*
> *I will be there.*

Everyone gathers at the end of the day to swap stories.

CHEETAHS BY THE NUMBERS

- Number of cheetahs worldwide in 1900: about 100,000

- Number of countries with cheetahs 100 years ago: 44

- Number of countries where cheetahs have since gone extinct: about 20

- Number of cheetahs alive today in the wild: about 10,000

- Number of cheetahs living wild in Iran (the only country outside Africa where they are found): less than 100

- Number of cheetahs living in zoos worldwide: about 1,500

- Percentage of the wild cheetah population living in Namibia: 20

- Times a week a cheetah must kill prey to stay healthy: about 2

- Times a week a cheetah is fed at CCF: 6 (they fast on Sundays)

- Land area, in square kilometers, of hunting territory of a coalition of males: in Namibia, 800–1,500; in East Africa: 38–48

- Average weight of a cheetah in pounds: 90–130

- Average weight of an African leopard in pounds: 120–200

- Average weight of an African lion in pounds: females, 265; males, 420

- Average age to which cheetahs live: in captivity, 10–12 years; in the wild, 8–10 years

- Percentage of wild cheetahs that die before 3 months of age in the Serengeti: 90

- Number of captured cheetahs returned to the wild by CCF: more than 600

- Number of Namibian kids in school groups that visit CCF headquarters each year: 2,000

Ignatius, Laurie, and the students of Rogate Primary School sing the cheetah song.

When Ignatius Davids was growing up in Otji-warongo twenty years ago, "animals meant danger," he told us.

"Be careful of warthogs! Snakes are poisonous! Cheetahs can kill you!" That's what he heard from his mom, a cook; his dad, a policeman; his neighbors; and even his teachers. But today, as an environmental educator with CCF, Ignatius says, "We want to change that to 'Oh, the animals are so beautiful! There is so much stuff to see!'"

Along with Ignatius, now thirty-one, and Laurie, we're on our way to help make that change. On our last day in Namibia, we're headed to Rogate Primary School in Otji-warongo, about a forty-minute drive from the CCF center.

Under the school's tin roof, inside its cement-block classrooms, the kids work at wooden tables and the teachers write on blackboards with chalk. There are no computers in sight. But there's plenty of learning. Every student here speaks at least two languages—English, the country's official tongue, and the local click language, Khoekhoegwab (pronounced "quay-quay go-vab"), in which many words include a

Natural science is an important subject in Namibian schools. The classrooms are unheated, so on cold days kids keep their jackets, hats, and gloves on inside.

Laurie loves to spend time encouraging the next generation of conservationists.

popping sound, made by snapping the tongue at the roof of the mouth. And in addition to English, math, and social studies, all the kids study natural science—in which conservation is now the major emphasis.

That's because Namibia's leaders understand, thanks in no small part to Laurie's work, that safeguarding their nation's natural treasures—including its cheetahs—is crucial to the country's future. "Once, you grew up to be a farmer, a doctor, a firefighter," says Ignatius. "But now, many of these kids will grow up to be an ornithologist, a tour guide, a veterinarian, an ecologist—maybe even a cheetah keeper!"

In grade seven, the twenty-six students already know Laurie and Ignatius well. "How do you say 'cheetah' in your language?" Laurie asks the class.

"*!Kharub!*" everyone answers. (The *!* means the word starts with a click. The rest of the word is pronounced "ah-ROOB.")

"Do you know who we are?" Laurie asks. "Cheetah Conservation Fund!" the students cry in unison. Laurie and Ignatius visit this school several times a year, giving lessons and handouts, including calendars with colorful pictures of cheetahs and other wildlife, and maps of Africa and the world.

In grade six, Ignatius holds up a map of

Giraffes use their long necks to reach high and browse. They consume about seventy-five pounds of leaves and twigs a day.

Africa. "The orange part shows where cheetahs used to live," says Laurie. Almost the entire continent is orange. "Now they are only in the red areas." There are only a few areas in red—mostly in Namibia, Botswana, Kenya, and Tanzania.

"So many animals on our earth today are in danger," she tells the students. "Elephants. Rhinos. Cheetahs. We have to take care of them. And Namibia is the cheetah capital of the world!

"Most cheetahs live on farmland," Laurie continues. "How many of you live on farms?"

About half the class raises hands.

"I grew up on a farm," Laurie tells the kids. "And I love my goats. I don't want anything to happen to them. That's why we have to teach you—and you have to teach your parents—how to take care of them."

Ignatius writes the word *predator* on the green blackboard in chalk. For every child in the class, English is a second or maybe even a third language. But a girl in a yellow necklace knows the word well and reads it perfectly. Ignatius tests the class: do they understand who the predators are?

They do. They point to photos of jackals and leopards, African wild dogs and cheetahs. "Do they eat vegetables?" Ignatius asks. The kids laugh and shout "No!"

They review. Yes, predators eat meat—pref-

erably wild game. They know these predators would rather not eat their livestock. They understand that as good stewards of their farms, they can use guarding dogs and shepherds to protect their flocks. And they have learned that if they are good stewards of the land, there will be plenty of wild duiker, steenbok, warthogs, and oryx for the predators to eat.

The class concludes with a song. The students know it well. They sing it in the round, creating a lovely harmony. The first lines go: "There is a cheetah! Can you tell me what a cheetah is?"

These kids sure can.

Ignatius remembers the first day he came to this school to talk to kids, many years ago. "I asked the kids, 'Who's afraid of predators?' All the little hands went up," he recalls.

"At the end of the day," says Ignatius, "from kids who were afraid of animals, I'll hear 'Now I'll tell my brother not to kill birds.' Or 'I'm going to ask my dad not to shoot cheetahs.' Kids do have the biggest power to change the world!"

The afternoon before the school visit, Laurie and her dad, Bruce, and Nic and I took the Land Rover out for a game drive. We watched two giraffes using their long, blueish tongues to reach between thorns and pluck acacia

leaves to chew. Oryx ran from us, then turned to stare, every face forward, swishing horselike tails. We saw warthog mothers trotting, tails high, leading their piglets to safety.

As the red sun was about to drop like a hot stone below the horizon, we saw something big in a tree. We raised binoculars and crept forward in the car. We gasped. On a low branch stood a huge bird, more than two feet tall, with a white mask, short, dark ear tufts, and black

At twilight we spotted a giant eagle owl, resting with its prey.

marks around its eyes. It was a giant eagle owl—one of the largest owls on earth—with a wingspan of four and a half feet. And what was it sitting on? "A nest?" Laurie's dad wondered. We crept closer until our truck was perhaps thirty yards away. That was no nest. The material at the owl's feet was the spotted black and white feathers of a guinea fowl it had just captured for dinner. No wonder the owl wasn't flying away!

The huge bird looked at us fearlessly. Through our binoculars, we could see that its eyes were big and orange, like twin suns. Its stare reminded me of the eyes of the cheetah—

and of something I had read before we came to Africa. "The cheetah gives me a feeling that is a mystery, no matter how much I learn about it," the biologist Randall Eaton wrote in his 1974 book *The Cheetah*, about his studies in East Africa. "It seems to look through me rather than at me. Its concerns seem to be honest and pure concerns of a quiet, graceful beast whose domain is its alone." Predators both, the owl and the cat once ruled their realms here in Africa. But now all of Africa's great predators teeter on the edge of a new era. They face either extinction or the dawn of resurrection. Which will it be?

"Cheetahs are survivors," Laurie had told us earlier. "They have survived for thousands of years. But if they are to survive, we have to be brave enough to make it happen."

At dinner, when we shared news of the owl sighting, several people noted that the owl is an ancient symbol of wisdom. Another mentioned a Native American legend that says when you see an owl, it means a change is coming. For Laurie, seeing the owl was like a promise: that yes, with the help of her human and animal staff, with the help of CCF's supporters around the world, with the help of the children whose schools she visits and maybe even with *your* help after you read this book—we can save the cheetah and change the world.

Around the fire that night, Laurie said, "Be the change you want to create." Then she thought for a minute. "That's a big owl. It must mean a big change."

LAURIE'S ADVICE FOR SAVING THE WORLD

1. "Don't wait for 'somebody' to do it. You can do anything!" It doesn't matter if you try something and fail, says Laurie—at least you've figured out that's not the right way to go. "My dad says I've never known what no means. I always think no is the other side of yes." How do you turn no into yes? "Never think you've failed. Always plan, and if you plan, take action. Don't be afraid to take that first step. If you keep stepping, all the right steps will go forward."

2. Never forget: "Animals need our help. If you don't take care of them, they'll go away." But today, she says, most people don't understand animals. "They don't understand that animals need habitat to get food, and if they have no food they'll die. We have the power to let that happen—or prevent it."

3. First we need to understand the basics of biology and the intricacies of biodiversity. "We're not alone!" says Laurie. "We should learn that before we can walk and talk. We should learn how to have 'interpersonal' relationships not only with humans but with nature, before we are allowed a certificate that says we're human. If we don't learn that, we're inhuman."

4. Get the facts. "Many problems are caused by not understanding. People might not be dumb, but they don't have the knowledge. Once they get the knowledge, then they can choose how they use it. The way they use it can be right or wrong, and if it's right they can feel good. But if they know the truth and do wrong—that will burn inside of them for a long time, and they'll become their own enemy."

5. "We can save the world. There's no reason we can't. But we have to actively do it." Young people like you have a huge part to play, Laurie stresses. "Children are influential. Young people can tell other people to do things. They can influence purchases. They can influence what their parents' businesses do. And if every child donated a dollar to the Cheetah Conservation Fund, they could save the cheetah. They could save every other species there is!"

Hi-Fi peers into the lens of a camera trap.

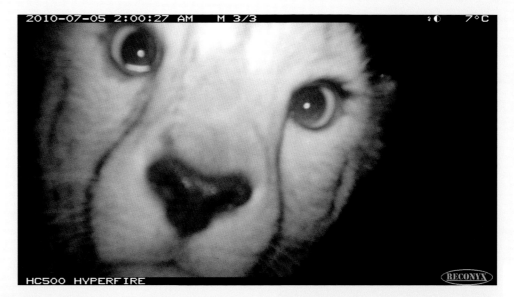

2010-07-05 2:00:27 AM   M 3/3   7°C

HC500 HYPERFIRE   RECONYX

Laurie scans the horizon for wildlife.

Bibliography and Resources

🐾 Adamson, Joy. *Pippa the Cheetah and Her Cubs.* New York: Harcourt, Brace & World, 1970.

🐾 Caro, T. M. *Cheetahs of the Serengeti Plains: Group Living in an Asocial Species.* Chicago: University of Chicago Press, 1994.

🐾 Eaton, Randall. *The Cheetah: The Ecology, Biology and Behavior of an Endangered Species.* New York: Van Nostrand Reinhold, 1974.

🐾 Marker, Laurie, D. Kraus, D. Barnett, and S. Hurlbut. *Cheetah Survival on Namibian Farmlands.* Windhoek, Namibia: Cheetah Conservation Foundation, 1996.

🐾 Williams, Lizzie. *Namibia Handbook.* London: Footprint Travel Guides, 2010.

🐾 Wrogmann, Nan. *Cheetah Under the Sun.* Johannesburg: McGraw-Hill, 1975.

The Cheetah Conservation Fund's official website, www.cheetah.org, is a treasure trove of information for conservationists, teachers, and kids. See great videos, read blogs from the field, get updates on the Ambassadors and other cheetahs, and visit a special section for kids (CheetahKids.com). To find out how to visit CCF yourself, go to cheetah.org/?nd=visiting _ccf_namibia. To learn more about volunteer opportunities and internships, visit cheetah .org/?nd=volunteer.

Additional Photo Credits

PAGE(S):

18 (top and bottom): Laurie Marker

19 (left and right), 26 (left and right), 29, 37 (bottom), 75: Cheetah Conservation Fund

Laurie and her husband,
Bruce, with the Stars.

Acknowledgements

It was a joy working with Dr. Laurie Marker, her parents, her staff, and the cheetahs, dogs, parrots, and goats at CCF in Namibia. In addition to all the individuals you've met in these pages, many others helped us enormously, and we want to thank them here. They are Anja Bradley, Niki Rust, Patricia Tricorache, Ludvig Swartz, Shannon Miller, Judy Wiseke, Paul Horgan, Lexi Decker, Joey Tarantino, Greg Noordanus, Peter Rabogliatti, Samantha Napolitano, June Kramer, Judith and Robert Oksner, and Jody Simpson.

CCF wouldn't be the marvelous organization it is without the hard work of many others we unfortunately didn't get to meet during our stay in Namibia. We wish to acknowledge Dr. Anne Schmidt-Kuntzel, director of CCF's genetics lab, as well as CCF's dedicated board of directors, trustees, and scientific advisors, as well as volunteers and supporters from around the world.

As always, Nic and I thank our wonderful editor, Kate O'Sullivan, our talented designer, Cara Llewellyn, and our understanding spouses, Vivien Pybus and Howard Mansfield.

And a special thanks to Carol Hosford, who, along with our friend Lisa Dabek (about whose work we wrote *Quest for the Tree Kangaroo,* also in this series), introduced me to Laurie in Seattle five years ago, and paved the way for this book.

SCIENTISTS IN THE FIELD
Where Science Meets Adventure

Check out these titles to meet more scientists who are out in the field—and contributing every day to our knowledge of the world around us:

Looking for even more adventure? Craving updates on the work of your favorite scientists, as well as in-depth video footage, audio, photography, and more? Then visit the new Scientists in the Field website!

www.sciencemeetsadventure.com